Niagara Cooks

from farm to table by Lynn Ogryzlo

W9-DBG-047

A delicious adventure

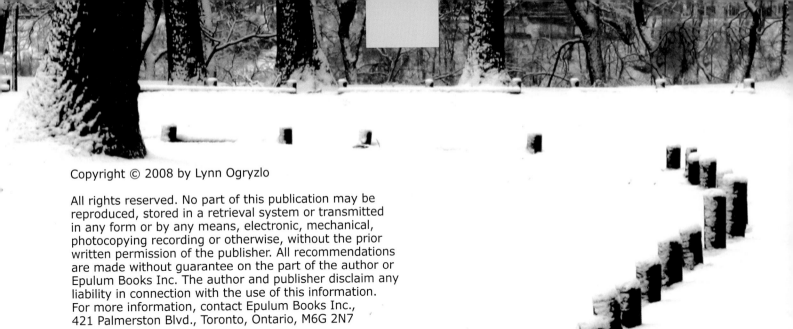

Copyright © 2008 by Lynn Ogryzlo

All rights reserved. No part of this publication may be
reproduced, stored in a retrieval system or transmitted
in any form or by any means, electronic, mechanical,
photocopying recording or otherwise, without the prior
written permission of the publisher. All recommendations
are made without guarantee on the part of the author or
Epulum Books Inc. The author and publisher disclaim any
liability in connection with the use of this information.
For more information, contact Epulum Books Inc.,
421 Palmerston Blvd., Toronto, Ontario, M6G 2N7

Published by Epulum Books Inc., Canada
Written by Lynn Ogryzlo
Edited by Molly Harding
Photographed by Jon Ogryzlo
Cover and interior design by Joan Crawford Graphic Design
Library and Archives Canada Cataloguing in Publication

Niagara Cooks, A delicious adventure
Lynn Ogryzlo: Includes recipes based on local produce,
stories on growers, sources for buying local and index
ISBN 978-0-9810031-0-8
1. Cooking 2. Agricultural Guide

Printed and bound in Canada by Friesens

The publisher and author acknowledge the support
of the 'Buy Local Champions' listed on page 184-187.
These innovative and enterprising leaders made
it possible to have this book printed in Canada.

Niagara Cooks

contents

I have had the pleasure of working with Lynn since our days at Inniskillin Wines. Lynn has always been a champion of regional cuisine and has built her journalism career promoting the wealth of Niagara's food and wine. It makes sense then for Lynn to embark on her first book about the Niagara Region's great wines and delicious foods. But this book takes readers an extra mile. Besides being a cookbook, with unique and delicious recipes for every meal and every season, Lynn also reveals the sources of Niagara's best local foods, and relates stories of the people who grow them.

The focus on local food is as refreshing as it's healthy, something becoming more and more important to us as Canadians. If you are particular about where your food comes from and want to prepare creative dishes, then *Niagara Cooks* should be in your kitchen. These pages are as full of seasonal inspiration, as Niagara fields are laden with produce. Let the bo take you through rural Niagara in search of the best tomatoes, peaches or strawberries. Learn about the people who grow the they'll share with you their natural family farming methods.

Niagara Cooks is Niagara's answer to the 100-Mile Diet, aiming to revitalize consumers' interest in the food grown in their own backyard. Niagara Cooks can bridge the modern-day gap between farmers and consumers, building relationships and providing the communities of Niagara with a source of safe, healthy food while nurturing the vibrant local economies in which we can all thrive.

Lynn backs-up her belief in Niagara produce by defining its unique characteristics and that of the region. Each expresses a sense of place or 'appellation' as we refer to it in the wine business. Local Food is the 21st century expression of 'terroir' – something important for taste and freshness and also for food safety.

For the ultimate experience, carry your *Niagara Cooks* with you as you tour the Niagara Culinary Trail. Whether you're from this great region, from other parts of Canada or from more distant shores, Lynn's book will get you started on enjoying Niagara's agri-tourism.

The publication of *Niagara Cooks* is perfectly timed. I look forward to trying some of the recipes along with my favorite VQA wines, which Lynn so masterfully pairs with each recipe.

Donald Ziraldo

This book is dedicated to the farmers of Niagara who provide us with fresh, healthy, delicious food.

I have been Niagara's food writer for more than a decade. Born into an Italian family that filled the entire yard with one big garden. If we weren't gardening, we were working on a farm, living the summer off seconds, canning and preserving for the leaner winter months. The fall was for wine and sausage making, while the winter months were occupied with bread and pasta making. Every season of the year had a food purpose.

When you live this life, food and cooking are more than just filling your stomach. It's a way to bring joy and love into your life and connect you to your surroundings. I can't remember a time when standing in the kitchen cooking over a stove, dining with friends or walking through the garden in search of another ripe tomato didn't make me happy. The creativity that goes hand in hand with food preparation calms me and brings a sense of belonging to my world that grounds me.

Even though I work in the kitchen alone, it's the sharing of good food with family and friends that inspires me. Sharing is the root of cooking and it's brought joyous memories and established culinary traditions for my family and friends; memories and traditions that have built a great life.

Obviously, it's all about where I live. I am especially lucky to live in the Niagara Region, where the soil and climate are ideal for producing some of North America's most flavourful foods. Here, we are rich in agricultural resources. We see orchards and vineyards everywhere. We can stop by the markets, talk to the farmers and drop by a roadside stand for whatever was harvested that day. How lucky we are to be so connected to our food!

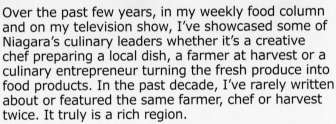

Over the past few years, in my weekly food column and on my television show, I've showcased some of Niagara's culinary leaders whether it's a creative chef preparing a local dish, a farmer at harvest or a culinary entrepreneur turning the fresh produce into food products. In the past decade, I've rarely written about or featured the same farmer, chef or harvest twice. It truly is a rich region.

Because I know as much, or perhaps more, about wine as I do about food, it was easy for me to select some of Niagara's greatest VQA wines to complement the foods. I hope you enjoy my recommendations. They're made to enrich the experience as perfect food and wine partners should.

This book is a new adventure for me and my multitalented photographer husband, Jon. He makes me laugh, inspires me and makes my work in the kitchen meaningful. I am incredibly excited to have worked with him on this project, for his talent is a gift and life together is a delicious journey.

This cookbook is by no means a full account of the dedicated growers, creative chefs or culinary artisans who contribute so much to Niagara, but it is a good place from which to begin your delectable adventures. Flip through the pages and I'll guide you through Niagara's culinary roadmap with recipes and techniques, local stories, introductions to farmers and flavourful possibilities. Through your journey I wish you many, many savoury adventures, memories and traditions of the most delicious kind.

. . .and so, it begins . . .

Niagara provides

What is now a firmly entrenched and recognized regional cuisine began to attract attention in the early '90s. Stephen Treadwell, executive chef of the Tiara Dining room at Niagara-on-the-Lake's prestigious Queen's Landing Inn, and a handful of other like-minded culinary pioneers were attracted to the region's wealth of incredible home-grown produce. They broke new ground serving local dishes with tremendous respect, preserving their lush goodness by cooking them with a minimum of fuss or embellishment.

Others followed and now in addition to Treadwell's own restaurant, Farm to Table Cuisine, Niagara boasts such amazing restaurants as Wellington Court Café, de Luca's at the Oban Inn, the Old Winery Restaurant, Queenston Heights, Vineland Estates, On The Twenty, Riverbend Inn and Vineyard, Peller Estates, Hillebrand Winery Café, AG@Sterling Inn, and many, many more. The chefs and owners of these establishments have pledged to use fresh local ingredients in support of local farmers and food processors, creating innovative dishes while reflecting Niagara's culinary terrior.

Niagara has deep roots in agriculture and a 'taste of place' with its food. Unlike other agricultural regions, Niagara has perfect geography and climate conditions that support the production of tender fruit, wine grapes and a wide variety of vegetables. They are all grown in the same soils and enjoy similar climate and geographical influences lending our fruit and vegetables unique flavours that are vibrant and intense -- a true taste of a Niagara summer.

Niagara farmers, the stewards of our land, nurture tiny seedlings into fully mature plants and raise livestock and poultry with natural farming methods to create pure, clean, exciting flavours – an undisputable quality and wealth of Niagara's bounty. This exciting explosion of Niagara artisan farmers is turning out some of the finest foodstuffs currently produced in the country.

Each harvest and every food has a celebration such as strawberry, cherry, peach, poultry and sausage festivals offering food traditions. Oh what delight you'll find in Niagara cherry pies, peach chutney, pumpkin doughnuts, roasted organic chicken on a bun and strawberry funnel cakes.

The Niagara Culinary Trail and the several county fairs showcase the mix of grand agricultural traditions and current taste innovations, from sheep shearing to heirloom vegetables, from maple tarts to preserves competitions. The region's food climate has even fostered unique businesses such as the Organic General Store, Tree and Twig Heirloom Vegetable Farm, and Winfield Farms, which offer its customers the luxury of having local and organic foods delivered to their homes.

Farmers markets continue to grow in number and size because no one can resist the sight of mounds of ripe heirloom tomatoes or buckets of just-picked cherries. Even local supermarkets are becoming excited and beginning to take pride in selling extremely fresh local produce.

Drive outside the city and you'll find plenty of roadside farm stands, with an "honesty box" tin can in which you must deposit your money. This is the simplicity and trust implicit in farm life. It's mostly here in the back roads where you'll find the artisan food movement thriving; the grinding of flour and corn, cheese and sausage makers, poultry and meat farmers, and the maple syrup, honey, preserves, vinegars and creative foodstuffs of all kinds.

Niagara is a prolific wine region, with more than 80 wineries ranging from large, sophisticated leaders in the world wine industry to small family owned and operated farm wineries producing small barrel batches of wine from their barns. This diversity gives us the perfect accompaniment to every meal and turns exquisite flavours into the ultimate dining experiences.

Niagara Cooks is rooted in the firm belief that "eating local", seasonally and sharing food together is one of the great and simple joys available to us all.

CHAPTER

1

page 11

Niagara Cooks is about culinary culture, regionalism and having a healthy sense of pride in our agricultural heritage.

apricot lavender coffee cake

2 1/4 cups (560 mL) all-purpose flour
1/2 cup (125 mL) lavender scented sugar
2 1/2 teaspoons (12.5 mL) baking powder
1/2 teaspoon (2.5 mL) salt
3 tablespoons (45 mL) unsalted butter, chilled
and cut into small pieces
1 tablespoon (15 mL) fresh lavender flowers
    (or 1 teaspoon (5 mL) dried)
1/2 cup (125 mL) whole milk
1 farm fresh egg, lightly beaten
1/2 cup (125 mL) apricot jam
4 tablespoons (60 mL) dried apricots, chopped
1/2 cup (125 mL) hazelnuts, chopped
Cooking oil
1 1/2 teaspoon (7.5 mL) sugar

Preheat oven to 375F (190C).
Combine flour, sugar, baking powder
and salt in a bowl.
Cut in butter with a pastry blender until mixture
resembles coarse meal. Stir in lavender flowers.
Add milk and egg, stirring just until moist.
Turn dough out onto a lightly floured surface.
Knead 5 times. Roll into a 9 x 7-inch rectangle.
Mix dried apricots and hazelnuts into preserves.
Spread apricot preserve mixture over dough,
leaving a 1/2-inch border. Beginning with long side,
roll up jelly-roll fashion; pinch seam to seal
(do not seal ends of roll).
Form roll into a circle and cut roll into
nine 1-inch slices.
Twist each slice, cut sides up, in an 8-inch non
stick round baking pan lightly coated with oil.
Sprinkle the slices with sugar.
Bake for 35 minutes or until golden brown.
Makes 1 ring.

CHAPTER

1

SERVES:
8 to 10

SEASON:
August

SERVE WITH:
A chilled glass
of sparkling
wine infused
with apricot
nectar

page 13

Grower Laura Kozloski has a love affair with lavender.
Owner of the Organic General Store in Niagara-on-the-
Lake, she has two plots of lavender in successful
production, one in Vineland, the other in Virgil.
In the store you'll find culinary lavender that is absolutely
fantastic, steeped in warm milk to make lavender ice
cream, infused in a simple syrup to add decadence to
strawberry ice tea or sprinkled over
lamb and pork dishes.

Organic General Store,
Niagara-on-the-Lake,
www.theorganicgeneralstore.com

DeCew blueberry cornbread

1 1/2 cups (375 mL) all-purpose flour
1 1/2 tablespoon (22.5 mL) baking powder
1/2 teaspoon (2.5 mL) salt
1 1/2 cups (375 mL) yellow cornmeal
6 tablespoons (90 mL) sugar
1 1/2 cups (375 mL) whole milk
1 farm fresh egg, beaten
3/4 cup (180 mL) unsalted butter, melted
1 cup (250 mL) market blueberries
maple syrup

Preheat oven to 425F (220C).
Butter a 12-inch cast iron skillet.
In a medium bowl, combine flour,
baking powder, salt, cornmeal and sugar.
Whisk to blend.
In a separate bowl, combine milk,
beaten egg and butter.
Pour the wet ingredients over dry mixture.
Stir to blend then fold in the blueberries.
Pour batter into skillet and bake for about
45 to 50 minutes.
Cool corn bread for 10 minutes before serving.
Turn out onto rack to cool completely.
Serve in slices drizzled with maple syrup.
Makes 1 loaf

CHAPTER

1

SERVES:
8 to 10

SEASON:
July, August
and if your
lucky,
September

SERVE WITH:
Cappuccino
and the
morning
paper

The only operating water-powered gristmill in the Niagara
Peninsula, Morningstar Mill produces authentic stone ground,
whole-wheat flour, bran flour, corn meal, corn flour and rye
flour in the traditional way. Morningstar Mill is also a museum
so visitors can tour the beautiful old historic mill, watch how
the grains are stone ground and purchase some product.
Because it's a water-powered gristmill, it's built on the side
of one of Niagara's most beautiful little waterfalls.
Plan a nature walk through the surrounding woods.

Morningstar Mill, Thorold,
www.morningstarmill.ca

buttermilk scones with Niagara jam

1 1/4 cups (310 mL) milk
1/4 teaspoon (1 mL) white vinegar
3 cups (750 mL) all-purpose flour
2 tablespoons (30 mL) baking powder
Pinch of salt
1/3 cup (80 mL) butter, melted
Milk
Sugar
Your favourite Niagara jam

Preheat oven to 400F (200C).
In a large measuring cup, put milk and vinegar and set aside for the milk to sour.
In a large mixing bowl, whisk together flour, baking powder and salt. Add melted butter and soured milk. Stir until a soft dough is formed.
Turn the dough out onto a lightly floured surface and press dough into a circle about 1-inch thick. Make slashes across the top of the scones to portion them into 8 even pieces.
Brush top with milk and sprinkle with sugar.
Place on a lightly greased baking sheet and bake for 20 to 25 minutes, or until golden brown. Serve with Niagara jam.

CHAPTER
1

SERVES:
8

SEASON:
May-June

SERVE WITH:
Morning coffee

Niagara Presents is a co-operative, community kitchen that helps aspiring culinary entrepreneurs develop delicious new food products from the fresh fruits and vegetables grown in the region. It's a government-inspected facility so people can formulate, prepare, bottle, and label unique recipes for jam, jellies, syrups, chutneys and more. The on-site retail store shelves are lined with different products all offering a flavour of the region from the quintessential Niagara condiment – peach salsa, to unique jam, fresh fruit toppings, spirited infusions and a complete line of wine jellies.

Niagara Presents, 4516 Mountainview Road, Beamsville, 905-563-1777 or 1-888-584-2387

Bluemin' double berry muffins

1 1/2 cups (375 mL) all-purpose flour
1/2 cup (125 mL) wheat germ
1/2 cup (125 mL) sugar
1 tablespoon (15 mL) baking powder
1/2 teaspoon (2.5 mL) salt
1 cup (250 mL) peach nectar
1/4 cup (60 mL) butter
1 farm fresh egg, lightly beaten
3/4 cup (180 mL) fresh blueberries
1/4 cup (60 mL) peach preserves

Preheat oven to 400F (200C).
Mix dry ingredients together and stir with a
whisk to blend.
Mix wet ingredients together and blend with the dry.
Mix until batter is just moistened.
Spoon half the amount of batter into 12
greased muffin cups.
Drop a teaspoon of peach preserves on the batter.
Add the blueberries to the remaining batter
and top up muffins.
Bake for 20 to 25 minutes or until edges
begin to brown.

SERVES:
12

SEASON:
June, July,
August

SERVE WITH:
Fruit
smoothie

Quality Fruit

Diana and Edward DiMarco purchased their blueberry
patch in 1997. They produce heavy crops of deep black,
large berries that are so luscious, the locals call them
'black pearls'. You can purchase DiMarco's black pearls
from the barn on the property and because they're sold
by weight, you can bring your own containers or use
the containers from the farm. So delicious are these
blueberries that some of the local bed and breakfasts
insist Diana bake blueberry muffins for their guests
– how lucky are they.

Bluemin' Acres, 905-468-8162
They have no computer nor website.

Niagara toast with caramelized rhubarb

4 farm fresh eggs
1/2 cup (125 mL) whole milk
2 tablespoons (30 mL) pure vanilla extract
1 tablespoon (15 mL) sugar
1/2 teaspoon (2.5 mL) ground cinnamon
Pinch of salt
8 thick slices country bread,
    about 1-inch thick

3/4 cup (180 mL) heavy cream
3/4 cup (180 mL) whole milk
1 vanilla bean
4 farm fresh egg yolks
4 tablespoons (60 mL) sugar

5 tablespoons (75 mL) unsalted butter
4 tablespoons (30 mL) Niagara honey
3 cups (750 mL) just-picked tart rhubarb,
    diced

In a shallow baking dish, lightly whisk together the eggs, milk, vanilla extract, sugar, cinnamon and salt.
Lay each piece of bread in egg mixture for 1 minute per side to soak up the egg mixture.
Meanwhile, combine half the cream and all of the milk in a saucepan.
Split the vanilla bean lengthwise and scrape the seeds into the milk, along with the bean.
Heat the mixture over medium high heat until small bubbles form around the rim, but do not boil.
Meanwhile, in a small bowl, whisk the remaining cream, egg yolks and sugar until smooth.
Dribble a bit of the hot milk mixture into the egg mixture, whisking continuously so the eggs don't curdle.
Continue adding until half of the hot milk has been incorporated.
Slowly pour the tempered egg yolk mixture into the saucepan with the remaining hot milk and cook over low heat, stirring constantly with a wooden spoon until the custard coats the back of a spoon, approximately 6 minutes.
Remove the vanilla bean and set mixture aside to cool.
Melt half the butter in a skillet over medium low heat and add the egg-soaked bread slices.
Cook until browned, approximately 3 to 4 minutes per side.
Transfer the French toast to an oven-proof plate as each slice is cooked and keep the slices warm in a 350F (160C) oven until all are cooked, approximately 10 minutes.
Meanwhile, heat the remaining butter in a saucepan with honey over medium high heat.
Stir and cook for one minute. Add rhubarb, cook until warmed through and soft, approximately 4 minutes.
Remove from heat.
To serve, place 2 slices of Niagara toast in the centre of each of 4 plates, top with vanilla cream and warm caramelized rhubarb.

CHAPTER
1

SERVES:
4

SEASON:
May,
June

SERVE WITH:
Konzelmann Estate Winery Sparkling Riesling with a rhubarb stock for garnish

page 23

There are no large commercial rhubarb growers in Niagara but there are plenty of artisan growers with small rhubarb patches. They supply local restaurants and sell at their fresh rhubarb at farmers' markets. Rhubarb also grows in backyards throughout Niagara, and there's a patch at the McFarland House on the Niagara River Parkway. Drop by the McFarland House and enjoy sugared rhubarb sliced and diced over scones or other casual fare in season. The sweetness of the sugar and the puckering sourness of the rhubarb is an exhilarating taste sensation.

pumpkin cider bread

1 1/2 cup (375 mL) apple cider
1 cup (250 mL) pumpkin purée
2 farm fresh eggs
1/4 cup (60 mL) Ontario canola oil
1/2 cup (125 mL) firmly packed brown sugar
1/2 cup (125 mL) grated Northern Spy apple
2 cups (500 mL) all-purpose flour
1 teaspoon (5 mL) baking soda
2 teaspoons (10 mL) double-acting baking
   powder
1/2 teaspoon (2.5 mL) salt
1/4 teaspoon (1 mL) ground mace
1/4 teaspoon (1 mL) ground cinnamon
Dash of ground cloves

In a saucepan, boil the cider until it is reduced
to about 1/4 cup (60 mL).
Remove from heat and let it cool.
In a bowl, whisk together the pumpkin puree, eggs,
oil, brown sugar, grated apple and the reduced cider.
In another bowl, whisk together flour, baking soda,
baking powder, salt, mace, cinnamon and cloves.
Add the flour mixture to the pumpkin mixture
and stir until just combined.
Transfer batter to a well-greased 8 x 4-inch loaf pan
and bake in a preheated 350F (180C) oven for
1 hour or until a tester comes out clean.
Remove from oven.
Let the bread cool.

SERVES:
8 to 10

SEASON:
October,
November

SERVE WITH:
Lincoln Line
Orchards
Sparkling
Cider

cream cheese icing

3 ounces (75 grams) cream cheese,
   room temperature
1 tablespoon (15 mL) butter,
   room temperature
2 teaspoons (5 mL) pure vanilla extract
2 tablespoons (30 mL) heavy cream
1/4 cup (60 mL) icing sugar

Combine cream cheese, butter, vanilla, cream and icing
sugar in a mixing bowl. Beat with an electric mixer until
smooth. Drizzle on cooled cider bread.
Makes 1 loaf.

It doesn't matter if you're looking for pumpkins to carve or
cook, you'll want to make your way to the Howell Family
Pumpkin Farm on Holland Road in Fonthill. October the farm
transforms itself into a giant interactive farm dedicated
entirely to pumpkins and pumpkin fun. The locals know not to
eat before they go, so they can treat themselves to an entire
dinner of grilled pumpkin sausages and warm pumpkin soup.
Then they can finish it off with a delicious piece of savoury
pumpkin pie rich with fall spices, and topped off with a scoop
of pumpkin ice cream. Don't forget to take away some
pumpkin donuts, they're a real seasonal tradition.

2878 Holland Road, Fonthill.
www.ahowlinggoodtime.com

pumpkin patch pancakes

1 1/2 cups (375 mL) whole milk
1 cup (250 mL) pumpkin puree
1 farm fresh egg
2 tablespoons (30 mL) Ontario canola oil
2 teaspoons (10 mL) white vinegar
2 cups (500 mL) all-purpose flour
2 tablespoons (30 mL) brown sugar,
    packed
2 teaspoons (10 mL) baking powder
1 teaspoon (5 mL) baking soda
1/2 teaspoon (2.5 mL) ground allspice
1 teaspoon (5 mL) ground cinnamon
1/2 teaspoon (2.5 mL) ground mace
1/2 teaspoon (2.5 mL) salt
White Meadow Farms Maple Syrup

In a bowl, mix the milk, pumpkin, egg,
oil and vinegar.
In another bowl, whisk together the flour,
brown sugar, baking powder, baking soda,
allspice, cinnamon, mace and salt.
Add the flour to the pumpkin mixture
and mix just enough to combine.
Heat a lightly oiled griddle over medium heat.
Pour the batter onto the griddle 2 tablespoons
(30 mL) at a time.
Let the pancakes cook until bubbles begin to
form on the top of the pancake.
Turn it over and cook for another 2 minutes
or until lightly browned.
Makes 24 pancakes.

CHAPTER

1

SERVES:
4

SEASON:
October,
November

page 27

HOW TO EAT LOCAL
The 100-Mile diet is an exercise in extremism designed
to make a point. But if you really want to eat local, it's
about doing the best you can. Take a look at your
grocery habits and find ways to switch a few local items
each week. Perhaps it's as simple as dropping into the
market before you hit the grocery store. Buy all you
can there and get the rest at the big stores. Once there,
always ask for Niagara products, read labels, and be
aware of the seasons. Each week you'll be able to find
more and more convenient ways to buy local produce.

farmhouse strawberry coffee cake

1 1/2 cups (375 mL) fresh market strawberries, washed, hulled and quartered
1/4 cup (60 mL) water
2 tablespoons (30 mL) cornstarch
3/4 cup (180 mL) milk
1/4 teaspoon (1 mL) white vinegar
2 1/4 cups (560 mL) all-purpose flour
3/4 cup (180 mL) sugar
3/4 cup (180 mL) unsalted butter, chilled
1/2 tsp (2.5 mL) baking soda
1/2 tsp (2.5 mL) baking powder
1 farm fresh egg, slightly beaten

Preheat oven to 350F (180C).
In a small saucepan, cook strawberries over medium-low heat until berries release liquid and are soft, about 5 minutes.
Combine water and cornstarch, mix well and add to strawberries.
Cook and stir until thickened and bubbly, about 2 minutes.
Remove from heat and set aside.
Add white vinegar to milk and set aside to sour.
In a large bowl, combine flour and sugar.
Cut in butter until the mixture resembles fine crumbs.
Remove 1/2 cup of the crumb mixture and set aside.
To remainder, add baking soda and powder.
Add egg to soured milk and mix to combine.
Add milk mixture to flour mixture.
Stir just to moisten.
Spread two thirds of the batter over the bottom of a 9-inch spring form pan.
With the back of a spoon, smooth batter out to edges of pan, making sure the batter touches the edges.
Spoon strawberry filling evenly on top.
Spoon remaining batter in small mounds on top of the strawberry layer.
Sprinkle the reserved crumb mixture on top.
Bake for 40 to 45 minutes or until golden on top.
Remove from oven and allow to sit for 10 minutes.

CHAPTER
1

SERVES:
8 to 10

SEASON:
May, June

SERVE WITH:
Champanade
Sparkling
Grape Juice

page 29

Niagara strawberries are so delicate that just by virtue of picking them you can bruise them; the flesh and juice 'cream' together under the weight of your finger. Just pick a ripe strawberry from a country patch and place it on your tongue. Now press up firmly against the roof of your mouth. The juice trickles over the sides of your tongue luxuriating the flesh as it gives way to release its intense flavour.

This is a Niagara strawberry moment.

As we crave different foods at different times of the year,
Mother Nature miraculously supplies us with the perfect ingredients
at just the right time.

It's the rhythm of the seasons.

lighter fare

CHAPTER

2

page 31

apple, butternut squash and beer soup

1 tablespoon (15 mL) Ontario Canola oil
2 cups (500 mL) onions, chopped
1 clove garlic, minced
1 teaspoon (5 mL) dried thyme
4 cups (1L) squash, peeled and chopped
3 cups (750 mL) McIntosh apples,
    peeled and chopped
2 cups (500 mL) chicken broth
2 cups (500 mL) Taps Premium Lager
1/2 cup (125 mL) table cream
Pinch nutmeg
Salt and freshly cracked black pepper
Apple slices for garnish

Heat oil in large soup pot over medium heat.
Add onions and cook about 5 minutes or until softened,
stirring occasionally.
Stir in garlic and thyme and cook 1 minute.
Add squash, apples, broth and lager.
Turn heat to high and bring to a boil, reduce heat and
simmer for about 15 minutes or until squash is tender.
Remove from heat and allow to cool.
Puree in small batches in blender or food processor.
Return puree to soup pot, add cream and reheat.
Season with nutmeg, salt and pepper.
Garnish with apple slices and serve warm.

CHAPTER
2

SERVES:
8

SEASON:
September,
October,
November

SERVE WITH:
Taps Brewery
Premium
Lager,
www.
tapsbeer.ca

page 33

Taps Brewery in Virgil is a family-owned microbrewery.
Chris Jefferies runs the place with his dad and
grandfather, brother-in-law and father-in-law. It's a
very small, hands-on operation that began in 2004 in
a small building on Walker Road in the Virgil business
park. It's here in a small quality operation they get
to play with flavours and local produce. They make
raspberry beer in June and peach beer in August.
They even make a wine barrel lager using old red
wine barrels.

www.tapsbeer.ca

Smithville smoked chicken pizza

1 ball of pizza dough from a neighbourhood
  bakery
1 teaspoon (5 mL) Ontario canola oil
1/2 cup (125 mL) tomato sauce
1 teaspoon (5 mL) smoke spice
1 cup (250 mL) smoked chicken meat from
  The Poultry Barn, diced
1/2 cup (125 mL) roasted red peppers, sliced
1 cup (250 mL) Mozzarella cheese, shredded
1 cup (250 mL) Niagara Gold cheese, cubed
2 tablespoons (30 mL) fresh parsley, minced

Put oil in a large bowl and coat pizza dough in the oil,
turning until it is completely coated.
Cover with a kitchen towel and let rest in a
warm place for an hour.
Preheat oven to 350F (180C).
Remove pizza dough from bowl and lay on a
lightly floured surface.
Roll into a 16-inch, thin circle with a rolling pin.
Lay the pizza crust on a circular pizza pan.
Mix tomato sauce with smoke spice and
spread on the crust.
Top pizza with chicken, red peppers,
cheeses and parsley.
Bake in the preheated oven for 25 minutes,
or until cheese is melted and bubbly.

CHAPTER

2

SERVES:
4

SEASON:
Spring,
summer,
winter, fall

SERVE WITH:
Harbour Estates
Winery Baco Noir,
www.
hewwine.com

page 35

Little does anyone realize, but Smithville and surrounding
area is the chicken capital of Ontario. Albert Witteveen is a
well-known chicken farmer with an on-site retail shop where
you'll find plenty of frozen chicken and, if you're lucky, you'll
also find a smoked chicken or two. Albert sends a few birds
down the road to Vic's Meats, a neighbourhood butcher (who
makes Niagara's best kielbasa) for smoking. Albert's smoked
chicken is absolutely delicious, with juicy meat and a
smokiness that turns savoury on the palate.

The Poultry Barn, 3133 Mountain Road, Grassie, 905-945-4329
Of course, chicken central is not complete without a festival
so you won't want to miss the Smithville Poultry Festival
held in June www.poultryfest.ca.

asparagus Parmesan tart

1 cup (250 mL) unbleached all-purpose flour
1/2 cup (125 mL) unsalted butter, chilled, cubed
1 3/4 cups (430 mL) finely grated Parmesan cheese
2 tablespoons (30 mL) ice cold water
4 tablespoons (60 mL) shredded Parmesan cheese
1 pound (450 g) asparagus, spears trimmed to 3 inches
1 cup (250 mL) half and half cream
2 farm fresh eggs
1/2 cup (125 mL) freshly grated Parmesan cheese
1 tablespoon (15 mL) chopped fresh tarragon
Salt and white pepper to taste

Preheat the oven to 350F (180C).
Place flour, butter and Parmesan in a food processor and pulse until butter is pea-sized.
With a few more pulses, blend in the ice water.
Transfer the dough into a 4 x 18-inch tart pan.
Working quickly, press the dough uniformly into the pan, pressing across the bottom and working towards the sides and up to form a rim.
Refrigerate and chill for 15 minutes.
Remove tart from the refrigerator and poke the bottom and sides a few times with the tines of a fork.
Line the tart with aluminum foil and fill generously with pie weights or dried beans.
Place on a baking sheet and bake for 15 minutes on middle rack of oven.
Pull the tart shell out of the oven, very gently peel back and remove the foil and pie weights.
Place the uncovered tart back in the oven and allow to cook for another 10 minutes, or until it is a deep golden brown.
Remove from the oven and sprinkle with shredded Parmesan.
Let cool to room temperature before filling.
Meanwhile, cook asparagus in boiling salted water till just crisp-tender, about 2 minutes.
Drain well. Place on paper towels.
Mix half and half, eggs, cheese, tarragon in a bowl.
Season with salt and pepper.
Arrange asparagus in tart and pour custard over.
Bake till tart puffs and top browns, about 35 minutes.
Cool slightly.

SERVES:
6

SEASON:
April, May

SERVE WITH:
Tawse Winery Carley's Block Riesling, www.tawsewinery.ca

In the early 1940s Niagara had dozens of asparagus growers and spring definitely had a different meaning. After disease hit, growers were advised to plant peaches in the sandy soil. Today, there is one asparagus growing operation that I know of, owned by Bill and Julie Johnston. On their farm at 3135 Tallman Drive, they have a small market garden that produces an amazing amount of spring asparagus. During asparagus season, Julie picks in the early morning and sells between 2 and 6 pm from her trailer on 21st Street between the Bailey Bridge and Culp Road. You can't get it any fresher than that!

Call for asparagus availability if there's none at the trailer, 905-562-5624

broccoli Parmesan soup

2 tablespoons (30 mL) unsalted butter
1 onion, chopped
4 cups (1 L) broccoli, separated into florets
   and stems
1 potato, peeled and chopped
6 cups (1.5 L) canned chicken stock, warmed
1/2 cup (125 mL) half and half cream
4 tablespoons (60 mL) freshly grated
   Parmesan cheese
Salt and freshly ground black pepper
1/4 cup (60 mL) sour cream
1 tablespoon (15 mL) table cream
Seasoned croutons
Shavings of Parmesan cheese

In a heavy-bottomed stockpot, melt butter and cook onion over medium heat until translucent, about 3 minutes.
Add broccoli and potato and cook for 5 minutes.
Add warm stock and simmer for approximately 10 minutes.
When potato and broccoli are tender, puree in batches in a blender or food processor.
Return to pot, add cream and Parmesan cheese and season to taste.
When ready to serve, spoon soup into individual bowls.
Mix sour cream and table cream together and drizzle over soup.
Garnish with seasoned croutons and Parmesan shavings.

CHAPTER

2

SERVES:
4
SEASON:
May, June

SERVE WITH:
Thirteenth Street Winery Cuvee Thirteen sparkling wine, www.13thstreetwines.com

page 39

LauRay Farms in Dunnville is owned by Laurie and Ray Korten. Laurie, a former chicken farmer, and Ray, a hog farmer, bought their farm 15 years ago and began a new venture of vegetable and fruit farming. On the 30-acre farm they grow a wide variety of vegetables from tomatoes and cucumbers to leeks, peas, brussels sprouts, garlic, peppers and of course, plenty of broccoli. LauRay broccoli is savoury and earthy with a depth flavour that fills the palate.

LauRay Farms, 1 Haldimand Road 17, Dunnville.
On-farm stand, Dunnville and Grimsby Farmers Market.

caramelized onion tart

4 tablespoons (60 mL) Ontario canola oil
5 large white onions, peeled and sliced thin
3 anchovy fillets
1 tablespoon (15 mL) dried thyme
2 cups (500 mL) all purpose flour
1/2 cup (125 mL) Ontario canola oil
1/2 cup (125 mL) whole milk, warmed
2 farm fresh eggs
4 tablespoons (60 mL) table cream
Salt and freshly cracked black pepper

In a large skillet, heat the oil and
sauté the onions, anchovies and thyme.
Cook stirring often until golden brown and very soft,
about 25 to 30 minutes.
Remove from heat and cool.
Meanwhile, combine flour, oil and milk in a
mixing bowl and mix well to form a soft dough.
Form into a ball, wrap in plastic wrap and chill for 10 minutes.
Preheat oven to 425F (220C).
Whisk eggs and cream and season with salt and pepper.
Pour egg mixture over cooled onions and set aside.
Roll out the dough to 1/4-inch thick and cut circles with
round cookie cutter to fit into tart shells or muffin tins.
Fill with onion mixture and bake for 30 to 35 minutes
until golden brown.
Serve warm or at room temperature.

CHAPTER

2

SERVES:
8

SEASON:
December,
January,
February

SERVE WITH:
Marynissen
Estate Cabernet
Merlot,
www.
marynissen.com

page 41

Lou Riklik of White Stag Orchards comes from a family
of farmers who tended mixed orchards and vineyards in
Eastern Europe. Carrying on the tradition, Lou was a
backyard orchardist before purchasing 8 acres in
Beamsville where he grows almost all of his produce
biodynamically, feeding the soil with natural materials to
increase the sugars and intensify the flavours. On the
orchard, the vegetable garden is called Maplekeys Kitchen
Gardens, and he specializes in heirloom and unique
varieties of lettuce, peas, carrots, beets, beans,
tomatoes, and onions.

White Stag Orchards, 3997 Green Lane Road, Beamsville.

Lakeshore chestnut pasta

1 tablespoon (15 mL) Ontario canola oil
1 tablespoon (15 mL) unsalted butter
1 garlic clove, minced
24 peeled roasted whole chestnuts
    from Grimo Nut Nursery
1 pound flat egg pasta such as tagliatelle
    or fettuccine
4 tablespoons (60 mL) finely grated
    Parmesan cheese
2 tablespoons (30 mL) unsalted butter
2 tablespoons (30 mL) finely chopped
    fresh flat-leaf parsley

Melt butter with oil in skillet over medium heat.
Add garlic and chestnuts and sauté for 1 minute,
being careful not to brown garlic.
Set aside.
Cook pasta according to package instructions, drain,
reserving 1/4 cup (60 mL) of pasta water.
Toss drained pasta with cheese, butter, parsley
and reserved pasta water.
Divide pasta among 4 dinner plates and garnish
with whole chestnuts.
Serve warm.

SERVES:
4

SEASON:
September to
December

SERVE WITH:
Chateau des
Charmes Gamay
Droit, St. David's
Bench Vineyard
www.
chateaudescharmes.
com

NIAGARA FOOD FESTIVAL
Celebrating its 15th year the 3-day food festival
features more than 40 restaurants, wineries and
food vendors offering delicious edibles to huge
crowds of hungry but happy participants. Loads of
casual foods reinvented, such as fresh cut fries with
sea salt and thyme, vintage flour grilled blue cheese
and pear in a cabernet baguette while farm fresh
corn on the cob boils away at a neighbouring stall.

Don't miss it every October in Welland,
www.niagarafoodfestival.com

cream of garlic soup

1 cup (250 mL) garlic cloves, peeled
3 tablespoons (45 mL) Ontario canola oil
2 cups (500 mL) chicken broth
1 cup (250 mL) dry chardonnay wine
2 cups (500 mL) milk
1 cup (250 mL) heavy whipping cream
1 potato, peeled and cubed
Salt and freshly cracked black pepper

Coarsely chop garlic.
Heat oil in a large saucepan over low heat.
Add the garlic and cook just until it begins to colour, stirring constantly.
Stir in chicken broth and wine and bring mixture to a boil.
Reduce heat and simmer for 30 minutes.
Stir in milk, cream and potato and simmer for another 30 minutes.
Remove from heat and allow to cool to room temperature.
In batches, puree soup in blender, return to saucepan and bring to a simmer. Season with salt and pepper to taste.
Ladle into bowls and garnish with a drizzle of extra virgin olive oil and garlic pods.

CHAPTER 2

SERVES:
6

SEASON:
winter

SERVE WITH:
Reif Estate Winery Chardonnay Reserve, www.reifwinery.com

page 45

George and Silvia Schurig decided to go back to their roots when they purchased a fruit orchard in Beamsville in 2008. They called it Edelweiss Orchards. On the farm they have more than 130 cherry, peach, apple, walnut and fig trees in addition to raspberries and rhubarb. They grow very few vegetables - a few tomatoes and an overabundance of pungent, juicy garlic that they just can't resist! George and Silvia are farmers with a taste for good food!

Edelweiss Orchard, 4366 Maple Grove Road, Beamsville, 905-562-3859.

field eggplant and onions

1 medium eggplant
2 teaspoons (10 mL) coarse salt
1/4 cup (60 mL) extra virgin olive oil
1 large white onion, thinly sliced
1 garlic clove, minced
Pinch of hot pepper flakes
1 teaspoon (5 mL) fresh oregano, chopped
Salt and freshly ground black pepper
1 tomato, cut into 8 slices
2 ounces (50 grams) Mozzarella cheese, sliced
Extra virgin olive oil
Balsamic vinegar

Trim eggplant and cut crosswise into 16 slices.
Sprinkle slices with coarse salt; place in colander to
drain for 30 minutes.
Rinse eggplant well under cool running water;
pat dry and set aside.
In skillet, heat 1 tablespoon of the oil over medium high
heat; cook onion, garlic and hot pepper flakes, stirring
often, for 3 to 5 minutes or until onion is softened.
Season with salt and pepper and set aside.
Heat 1 tablespoon of oil in the same skillet and cook
eggplant for 3 minutes or until slices are beginning
to brown.
Turn eggplant over and cook for an additional 3 minutes
or until edges begin to brown.
Add more oil if necessary.
Lay half the eggplant slices on a cookie sheet.
Top with tomato slices, onion mixture and another
slice of eggplant.
Top with Mozzarella slices and broil for 1 to 2 minutes
until cheese melts and begins to brown.
Serve 2 eggplant and onion stacks per plate drizzled with
a good quality extra virgin olive oil and balsamic vinegar.

CHAPTER

2

SERVES:
4

SEASON:
August,
September

SERVE WITH:
Creekside
Estate Winery
2001 Signature
Meritage,
www.
creeksidewine.com

Linda Crago of Tree and Twig Heirloom Vegetable Farm in
Wellandort is Niagara's queen of heirloom vegetables.
Most know her for the rich, juicy tomatoes she grows
– more than 400 varieties! Linda's garden is also full of
hundreds of other heirloom and exotic vegetables, rich in
flavour, all grown naturally. Her eggplant is exotic, her
onions, juicy and robust. Linda runs a Community Shared
Agriculture program and if you're lucky enough you may
get on her list. If not, buy from her farm stand or the
Fonthill Farmers Market, www.treeandtwig.ca

fresh tomato basil pasta

4 fresh garden tomatoes, diced
10 basil leaves, roughly chopped
2 spring onions, sliced
1 clove garlic, minced
1/4 cup (60 mL) extra virgin olive oil
Salt and freshly ground black pepper
1/2 pound (.23 kg) farfalle or orecchia pasta

Combine the first 5 ingredients in a bowl and season
with plenty of salt and pepper.
Set aside for the tomatoes to release their juices.
Meanwhile, cook the pasta according to package directions.
When pasta is al dente, drain and return hot pasta
to the empty pot.
Drain the juices from the tomato mixture into the pasta.
Toss until fully coated.
Transfer the pasta to a large serving bowl and top
with drained tomato basil mixture.

CHAPTER
2

SERVES:
2

SEASON:
August,
September

SERVE WITH:
Henry of Pelham
Winery Cuvee
Catharine, www.
henryofpelham.
com

page 49

Tomatoes define a Niagara summer. If you need any proof,
all you need do is eat a tomato in January - the taste
difference is enormous, which holds true even more so
for the heirloom tomatoes that are starting to appear in
supermarkets. Bite into a vine-ripened Niagara heirloom
tomato, and it bursts in your mouth with sweet, bright,
juicy tomato flavour that is overwhelmingly sensual and
seductive. Taking the feast-or-famine approach, live on
tomatoes from the moment they appear in the market
to the first killing frost - then none until next year.

Look for them at farmers markets throughout the region
and plan on attending the Niagara Bigga Tomatafest at
Queenston Heights Park in late August, 905-354-9342

garlic scape gnocchi with sage brown butter

1 pound (450 g) Ricotta cheese
2 egg whites
1/2 cup (125 mL) finely chopped garlic scapes
1 3/4 cups (330 mL) all-purpose flour
1 teaspoon (5 mL) salt
1/2 teaspoon (2.5 mL) freshly ground
    black pepper
1/3 cup (80 mL) butter
6 large cloves garlic, chopped coarsely
Leaves from 1 bunch fresh sage
Salt and freshly ground black pepper to taste
Fresh garlic scapes for garnish
Freshly grated Parmesan cheese for garnish

Place the Ricotta, egg whites and scapes in a food processor and process until scapes are minced.
In a medium-sized bowl, combine the flour, salt and pepper. Gradually add the dry ingredients to the Ricotta mixture and pulse just until blended. Add more flour if needed to form a dough that is moist yet not too sticky.
Turn out the dough onto a lightly floured work surface and divide into 8 balls.
Using your palms, roll each ball against the work surface into a rope approximately 1/2-inch in diameter.
Try not to overwork the dough or work too much flour into it or it will toughen.
Using a sharp knife cut off 1-inch pieces.
Place them on a flour-dusted baking sheet and cover with a clean kitchen towel.
Bring a large pot three-fourths full of water to a boil.
Meanwhile, in a sauté pan over medium heat, warm the butter until it begins to brown.
Add the garlic and most of the sage leaves and sauté for approximately 2 minutes or until the garlic is soft and the butter is browned but not burned. Season with salt and pepper. Keep warm.
Drop the gnocchi into the boiling water and cook for 3 to 5 minutes – they are cooked when they float to the surface.
Drain the gnocchi and place in a warm serving dish.
Pour the browned butter over the top and toss to coat.
Garnish with fresh sage leaves, scapes and grated cheese.
Serve warm.

Riverbend Inn & Vineyards is Niagara's only vineyard inn. Executive Chef Chris Smythe contracted grower Dave Perkins of Wyndam Farm to design a large kitchen garden adjacent to the herb garden at the back of the inn. Chef Smythe's specialty is wine country cuisine and he now has a garden filled with fresh produce that grows next to the vines. From garden to dish and vine to wine, the Riverbend Inn is a spectacular taste experience.

Riverbend Inn & Vineyard, 16104 Niagara River Parkway, Niagara-on-the-Lake, 905-468-8866

NOTE: If garlic scapes are difficult to find, you can substitute garlic chives.

CHAPTER
2

SERVES:
4

SEASON:
May, June

SERVE WITH:
Riverbend Inn
Chardonnay
Reserve,
www.
riverbendinn.ca

page 51

farmers' gaspacho

2 large tomatoes
1/2 English cucumber
1 slice red onion
1 green pepper, seeded and cut into quarters
2 garlic cloves
1 1/2 cups (375 mL) tomato juice
3 tablespoons (45 mL) extra virgin olive oil
Juice of ½ lemon
1 tablespoon (15 mL) apple cider vinegar
Fresh dill
Salt and freshly cracked black pepper
De la terra sourdough croutons

Put tomato, cucumber, onion, pepper and garlic cloves
in blender with tomato juice, olive oil, lemon juice,
apple cider vinegar and dill.
Purée until almost blended, leaving chunks
to give the soup texture.
Season with salt and pepper and refrigerate for 4 hours
or preferably overnight to blend the flavours.
Ladle cold soup into 4 bowls and serve with croutons.

CHAPTER

2

SERVES:
4

SEASON:
August,
September

SERVE WITH:
Hillebrand
Estates Winery
Trius Sparkling,
www.hillebrand.
com

De la terra Bakery in Fonthill is an organic bakery
specializing in big, dense, incredibly flavourful
sourdough breads. Thick slices of their bread make
great accompaniments to this bright soup, or you can
purchase croutons ready made from day-old bread.
Either way, de la terra sourdough bread is a must-have
gaspacho accompaniment.

De la terre café & bakery, 1455 Pelham Street, Fonthill.

heirloom tomato tarts

1 head garlic
1 teaspoon (5 mL) extra virgin olive oil
3/4 cup (180 mL) unsalted butter, chilled,
    cut into ¼-inch cubes
2 cups (500 mL) all-purpose flour
1 teaspoon (5 mL) salt

1/4 cup (60 mL) all-vegetable shortening,
    cut into 1/4-inch cubes
1 farm fresh egg, lightly beaten
3 tablespoons (45 mL) ice water
4 ½ ounces (113 grams) soft goats cheese,
    room temperature
12 fresh basil leaves, minced
Salt and freshly ground black pepper
20 tiny heirloom red tomatoes,
    halved lengthwise
20 tiny heirloom yellow tomatoes,
    halved lengthwise
Basil sprigs as garnish

Preheat oven to 425F (210C).
Slice the top off the garlic just to expose the tops of each clove. Place garlic on 6-inch square of foil and drizzle with olive oil. Seal foil packet and bake in oven for 45 minutes or until garlic is soft. To make the pastry, mix flour and salt in a food processor fitted with a steel blade.
Scatter butter pieces over flour mixture. Add salt.
Cut butter in with 5 1-second pulses.
Add shortening and cut into mixture with about 4 more 1-second pulses. The mixture should resemble coarse cornmeal, with butter bits no bigger than peas. Transfer mixture to a mixing bowl. Sprinkle ice water over flour mixture. Mix in with a fork until the dough sticks together. Add more ice water if the dough will not come together. Wrap dough in plastic and refrigerate for at least 30 minutes or up to 2 days before rolling out. When ready, roll the dough between two sheets of waxed paper lightly dusted with flour so it doesn't stick. Cut 6-inch circles and line the 4-inch tart tins. Prick the bottoms with a fork, line with foil and pie weights, bake for 15 minutes.
Remove pie weights and bake for another 10 to 15 minutes. Remove from oven and let cool.
Combine the goats cheese and basil in a mixing bowl. Squeeze the roasted garlic by laying the head on its side and pressing down with the blunt end of a knife.
Add the garlic to the goats cheese and mix until well combined. Season with salt and pepper.
Fill the cooled tarts with goats cheese mixture and arrange tomatoes in alternating colours around the tarts. Season with salt and pepper and garnish with a sprig of fresh basil.

Concerned about the rising costs of fuel and food, Vivek Rajakumar decided to farm. On the 13-acre Victory Herb & Farm, Vivek grows strawberries and salad greens using untraditional vertical farming methods and his specialty peppers, eggplant and other garden vegetables are grown in raised beds, hydroponics fashion. Vivek grows a lot of specialty products like the Chocolate Beauty Pepper that is bright green on the inside and black outside, he teaches classes on starting and managing your own back yard garden and he opens up his 13-acre farm to anyone wanting to pick the fresh produce themselves.

Victory Herb & Farm, 2100 Seventh Street Louth,
St. Catharines, open daily in season.

CHAPTER

2

SERVES:
6

SEASON:
August,
September

SERVE WITH:
Fielding Estate
Winery Rock
Pile Pinot Gris,
www.
fieldingwines.
com

page 55

Niagara Gold flans

3 tablespoons (45 mL) creamy butter
2 cups (500 mL) cooking onions, sliced
3/4 cup (180 mL) table cream
3 farm fresh eggs
Salt and freshly cracked black pepper
1 1/4 cups (310 mL) grated
   Niagara Gold cheese

Preheat oven to 300F (150C).
Place 6 ramekins or custard cups in a deep baking pan.
Set aside.
Melt butter in skillet over medium heat and add onions.
Sauté until tender but not brown, about 10 minutes.
Cool slightly and transfer to blender.
Add cream and eggs and blend until smooth.
Season with salt and pepper.
Divide cheese equally among the ramekins and pour onion mixture over.
Fill baking pan with enough hot water to come halfway up sides of the ramekins.
Bake flans until centres are softly set, about 30 minutes.
Cool flans 10 minutes in pan then finish cooling on baking rack.

CHAPTER

2

SERVES:
6

SEASON:
January
to March

SERVE WITH:
Vineland Estate
Winery Chenin
Blanc, www.
vineland.com

page 57

Niagara has only one artisan fromagerie and it's in the trendy village of Jordan Station. Upper Canada Cheese Company makes 3 different cheeses from top quality Guernsey milk from the Comfort's dairy farm in neighbouring St. Anne's. In the on-site gourmet retail shop you can find Niagara Gold, a Gouda-style cheese with earthy flavours and a dense texture; Comfort Cream, a Brie-style cheese with a creamy flavour and luscious mouthfeel; and Ricotta, produced from the whey leftover from the Niagara Gold and Comfort Cream. And if you're lucky, you can find it still warm in the refrigerated section of the retail shop.

Upper Canada Cheese Company,
www.uppercanadacheesecompany.com

country pasta

2 tablespoons (30 mL) unsalted butter
1/2 onion, minced
1/2 cup (125 mL) clear chicken stock
1 cup (250 mL) dry white wine
1 pound (.45 kg) spaghettini
1/2 cup (125 mL) fresh peas, out of pod
4 slices Pingue prosciutto, sliced
1 cup (250 mL) freshly grated Parmesan cheese
Salt and lots of freshly ground black pepper

Melt butter in a medium saucepan, add the onions and cook over low heat until onions are soft, about 4 minutes. Add the chicken stock and wine and bring to a boil. Lower heat and simmer for 3 to 5 minutes or until reduced by half.
Meanwhile cook the pasta in lightly salted boiling water according to package directions.
Add the peas and prosciutto to wine sauce and cook for 1 minute. Add half the Parmesan cheese.
Heat through, stirring.
Season to taste.
Drain pasta and transfer back into the warm pot.
Pour the sauce on the pasta and toss well.
Divide among 4 individual dinner plates and sprinkle with the remaining grated Parmesan.

CHAPTER
2

SERVES:
4

SEASON:
June, July

SERVE WITH:
Frogpond Farm
Organic Winery
Cabernet Merlot,
www.
frogpondfarm.ca

page 59

Mario Pingue immigrated from Salmona, Italy, and brought with him his love of his country's cured meats. He always made his own prosciutto, salami and sausages, so when he retired it seemed the natural thing to carry on. Restaurants can't get enough of Pingue meats; prosciutto, bresaola, salami, dried and fresh sausage and pancetta. All of the products are made naturally, using only organic meat. Many of the products are aged for 24 months, and all are cured with sea salt. Nitrates are never used in any of the products. You can buy Pingue meats at Cheese Secrets and Pairings Specialty Food Market in Niagara-on-the-Lake and at Olson Bakery and Foods in Port Dalhousie.

sherried onion and barley soup

2 tablespoons (30 mL) creamy butter
2 tablespoons (30 mL) Ontario canola oil
8 cups (2 L) cooking onions, sliced
1/3 cup (80 mL) pearl barley
3 tablespoons (45 mL) Joseph's Estate Wines
    Olde Niagara Cream Sherry
8 cups (2 L) chicken stock
4 fresh thyme sprigs
Salt and freshly ground black pepper

Melt butter with oil in heavy soup pot over
medium-high heat.
Add onions and sauté until caramelized, about 20 minutes.
Add barley, sherry, chicken stock and thyme and
bring to a boil.
Reduce heat, cover and simmer 30 minutes.
Remove from heat, discard thyme sprigs and
season with salt and pepper.
Serve warm with a fresh loaf of
country crusty bread.

CHAPTER
2

SERVES:
6

SEASON:
winter

SERVE WITH:
Joseph's Estate
Wines Olde
Niagara Cream
Sherry,
www.
josephsestatewines.
com

page 61

Joseph Pohorly was a civil engineer and amateur
winemaker when he decided to open Newark Wines in
1979. His new venture, Joseph's Estate Wines on Niagara
Stone Road is a true reflection of the winemaker and his
talents. In this little retail store you'll find fine table
wines, delicious fortified wines, succulent fruit wines and
grapeseed oil. There doesn't seem to be any part of the
grape that Joseph can't find a use for. Recently chef
Patrick Hogan approached Joseph on a new venture.
Together they take the leftover grape skins and make a
flour from them. The partnership is called Vintage Flour
Niagara and you can purchase it at the winery retail
store. They'll even give you recipes on how to use it.

Ridge Meadow sweet pea quiche

1 cup (250 mL) all-purpose flour
1/4 cup (60 mL) grated Parmesan cheese
1 tablespoon (15 mL) chopped fresh thyme
Pinch of salt
1/2 cup (125 mL) unsalted butter
1 farm fresh egg
2 strips smoked bacon, diced
1 1/2 cups (375 mL) fresh green peas
1 tablespoon (15 mL) torn fresh tarragon
4 farm fresh eggs, beaten
3/4 cup (180 mL) milk or heavy cream
Salt and freshly ground black pepper

Preheat oven to 400F (200C).
In a food processor, combine the flour, cheese, thyme and salt and process until well mixed.
Add the butter and process until the mixture is mealy.
Add the egg and process just until a firm ball gathers around the blade.
Roll out the pastry and use to line the base and sides of a deep 6-inch spring form or loose-based cake pan.
Prick the base of the pastry and chill.
Meanwhile, cook diced bacon in a heated skillet until crisp, approximately 4 minutes.
Drain on paper towels.
Sprinkle bacon over pastry base then add peas and sprinkle evenly with tarragon.
Whisk the eggs, milk, salt and pepper together and pour the mixture into the pie shell.
Cover loosely with foil and place in the oven.
After 20 minutes, remove the foil and continue to cook for an additional 25 minutes or until pastry is lightly browned.
Serve warm or cold.

CHAPTER
2

SERVES:
6

SEASON:
June, July

SERVE WITH:
Jackson-Triggs
Vintners
Sauvignon Blanc,
www.
jacksontriggswinery.
com

page 63

Beth Smith grows a variety of specialty vegetables on her 9-acre farm in Beamsville called Ridge Meadow Farm. Each year Beth plants more peas for the never-ending demand. She likes to grow Eclipse sweet peas that holds their sweetness longer after being harvested. This variety is also heat tolerant so the sweetness of the peas hangs on even after they're cooked. But most Niagarans find just-picked, sweet peas in the pod too irresistible and most are eaten as snacks before they even enter the kitchen.

You can meet Beth at the Niagara-on-the-Lake Farmers' Market and the Fonthill Farmers' Market.

Niagara chicken wraps

3 chicken breasts, boneless, skinless,
    sliced into strips
2 tablespoons (30 mL) soy sauce
2 tablespoons (30 mL) Ontario canola oil
Salt and freshly ground black pepper

1/2 seedless cucumber, julienned
1 carrot, peeled and julienned
1 cup (250 mL) fresh bean sprouts
1/2 cup cilantro leaves
2 tablespoons (30 mL) white vinegar
Salt

SPICY PEANUT SAUCE
1/2 cup (125 mL) dry roasted Ontario peanuts
4 tablespoons (60 mL) water
1 clove garlic, minced
1/4 teaspoon (1.5 mL) dark soy sauce
1 teaspoon (5 mL) sesame oil
2 teaspoons (10 mL) brown sugar
1 tablespoon (15 mL) fish sauce
1 teaspoon (5 mL) red chili sauce
    (more or less to taste)
1/2 teaspoon (2.5 mL) verjus

4 12-inch flour tortilla wraps

Heat a skillet over medium high heat.
Toss chicken with soy and oil and add to hot skillet.
Cook, turning, until chicken is no longer pink,
about 10 minutes.
Season.
Remove from skillet and set aside to cool.
Combine cucumber, carrots, sprouts and cilantro
leaves with a generous sprinkle of vinegar.
Season with salt to taste.
Place all peanut sauce ingredients in a blender.
Blend until sauce is smooth.
If you prefer a runnier peanut sauce, add a little more water.
Set aside.
Pile chicken and veggies in wraps and drizzle liberally with
spicy peanut sauce before wrapping and rolling tightly.
Serve extra peanut sauce on the side.

SERVES:
6

SEASON:
Spring,
summer,
winter, fall

SERVE WITH:
Charles Baker
Riesling,
www.
charlesbaker.ca

page 65

Charles Baker is Director of Marketing and Sales for
Stratus Vineyards and his passion is Riesling. Thanks to
the confidence, foresight and generosity of Stratus owners,
Charles has been experimenting and created some unique
Niagara Rieslings. These new wines are a 3-way powerhouse
partnership between Charles Baker, Mark Picone Vineyards,
winemakers J.L. Groux, and the entire team at Stratus
Vineyards which allows Baker to follow his dreams.

The wine is available at www.charlesbaker.ca and if you're
lucky, you can find a few bottles at Stratus Vineyards
on Niagara Stone Road in Niagara-on-the-Lake.

fire blackened red pepper soup

8 sweet red bell peppers
2 tablespoons (30 mL) Ontario canola oil
2 onions, chopped
3 garlic cloves, chopped
1 small hot red pepper, seeded and halved
2 teaspoons (10 mL) chopped fresh thyme leaves
6 cups (1.5 L) chicken broth
1 potato, peeled and coarsely chopped
1/2 cup (125 mL) dry white wine
Salt and freshly ground white pepper
Sour cream
Thyme leaves for garnish

Heat the barbecue and place the red peppers over the grill.
When the skin is blackened, turn peppers over.
Continue to char and turn until the entire pepper is blackened.
Remove from hot grill and put inside a paper bag, close tightly and set aside until cool enough to handle.
Place charred peppers on a cutting board.
Scrape off blackened skin with a knife.
Skin should fall off easily.
Remove stems and seeds.
Meanwhile, heat oil in a heavy large pot
over medium-high heat.
Add the onions, garlic, hot pepper and thyme and
sauté until the onions are translucent, about 5 minutes.
Add the broth, charred peppers, potato and wine.
Bring to a simmer over high heat.
Decrease the heat to medium low.
Partially cover and simmer until the potatoes are very tender, stirring occasionally, about 30 minutes.
Cool the soup slightly.
Working in batches, puree the soup in a blender, taking care not to overfill the blender.
Season the soup to taste, with salt and pepper.
Ladle the soup into bowls.
Place a dollop of sour cream in the centre of each bowl and top with a sprig of thyme.
Sprinkle with white pepper and serve.

CHAPTER

2

SERVES:
6

SEASON:
August,
September

SERVE WITH:
Lailey Vineyards
Gewurztraminer,
www.
laileyvineyard.
com

page 67

COMMUNITY SHARED AGRICULTURE (CSA)
Beyond the roadside stands and the farmers markets, there is another way locals can ensure their fair share of the limited Niagara harvests. Join a Community Shared Agriculture program and reserve a garden share. You'll receive weekly deliveries of freshly harvested produce from a local farm. In Niagara, Tree & Twig Heirloom Vegetable Farm, Winfield Farms and the Organic General Store all offer CSA programs.

Some are seasonal, others are year-round.
Check them out at www.NiagaraCulinaryTrail.com

It is in our agricultural community,
where we find the most valuable resources,
the greatest intensity of flavours
and the purest of produce.

farm market vegetables

CHAPTER

3

Cherry Lane orchard chutney

4 apples, peeled, cored and diced
1 cup (250 mL) dried cherries from
    Cherry Lane Orchards
2 cooking onions, peeled and minced
1 1/2 cups (375 mL) brown sugar
2 cups (500 mL) apple cider vinegar

Put the apples, cherries and onions in a large glass bowl.
Add the sugar and vinegar.
Stir very well and stir once a day for 3 days,
keeping the bowl covered with a kitchen towel.
Makes approximately 6 cups of chutney.

SERVES:
8 to 10

SEASON:
October,
November,
December

Cherry Lane is a 450-acre estate in Vineland farmed by 9th generation John and his daughter Jenifer Smith. Besides fresh picked, black sweet cherries, and red sour cherries, Cherry Lane also offers pails of frozen sour pitted cherries in 4 different sizes. They're absolutely fantastic for home bakers. Their specialty health product is cherry concentrate juice and a variety of dried fruit including cherries.

Cherry Lane, Victoria Avenue, Vineland,
www.cherrylane.net

field asparagus with buttered shallots

24 thin asparagus spears
3 tablespoons (45 mL) Ontario canola oil
1 tablespoon (15 mL) red wine vinegar
1/2 teaspoon (2.5 mL) Dijon-style mustard
Salt and freshly cracked black pepper
1 tablespoon (15 mL) butter
3 shallots, sliced paper thin
2 sundried tomatoes, diced
1 garlic clove, minced
1/2 cup (125 mL) crumbled goats cheese
8 pieces baguette, diagonally sliced

Snap the tough ends from each asparagus spear.
Fill a skillet with 1-inch of salted water and add asparagus.
Cook only until water comes to a boil.
Remove from heat, drain and rinse immediately under cold water.
Whisk together the oil, vinegar and mustard and season with salt and pepper.
Toss with asparagus until completely coated.
Set aside.
In a small skillet, melt butter and add shallots, sundried tomatoes and garlic.
Cook for 2 minutes or until shallots are soft.
Set aside.
Sprinkle goats cheese on each baguette slice.
Lay 3 asparagus spears on each and top with sundried tomato mixture.

CHAPTER

3

SERVES:
4

SEASON:
June

page 73

EAT LOCAL.
Foods grown in your own backyard are fresher and taste better than food shipped long distances from other parts of the world. Buying local is simply a matter of attitude. Grow it in your own backyard and if you can't, buy from Niagara farmers. Choose local over organic and when all else fails buy Fair Trade. Buying from local farmers keeps farmland part of our landscape, keeps farmers farming and builds healthy communities.

garden asparagus with horseradish pea puree

2 cups (500 mL) fresh peas
2 tablespoons (30 mL) sour cream
2 teaspoons (10 mL) prepared horseradish
1 tablespoon (15 mL) chopped fresh chives
Salt and pepper to taste
2 pounds asparagus spears

Bring a large pot of salted water to a boil.
Add peas and cook 3 to 5 minutes, or until tender.
Drain, reserving 1/4 cup cooking liquid.
Transfer peas to food processor.
Add sour cream, horseradish and reserved cooking liquid, and blend until smooth.
Season to taste with salt and pepper.
Snap the tough ends from each asparagus spear.
Fill a skillet with 1-inch of salted water and add asparagus.
Cook only until water comes to a boil. Remove from heat, drain and rinse immediately under cold water.
Arrange the asparagus in 4 folded napkins and place on 4 individual plates.
Place horseradish pea puree in mini ramekins, sprinkle with chives and serve on the side.

CHAPTER
3

SERVES:
4

SEASON:
June

Fifty years ago John Drope, a local businessman, saw the potential in an abandoned canning factory on the corner of King and John Streets. Inspired by the tourist draw the Shaw Festival Theatre commanded, Drope transformed the cannery into a colonial-style inn he named The Pillar and Post. The cannery was one of four at the time in Niagara-on-the-Lake; Union Jack Canning Company on Platoff Street, the Delhi Canning company dockside, the Niagara Canning Factory on Lakeshore Road (now houses Strewn Winery and the restaurant, Terroir La Cachette) and of course, Canadian Canners on the corner of King and John Streets. The Pillar & Post Inn and the Cannery Restaurant is where Aylmer products were made. Today Executive Chef Randy Dupuis honours the Inns heritage by using local products in his dishes.

Pillar & Post Inn, Cannery Restaurant, 48 John Street, Niagara-on-the-Lake, 904-468-2123
www.vintage-hotels.com

page 75

country corn with chive butter

1/2 cup (125 mL) unsalted butter,
   room temperature
1/3 cup (80 mL) finely chopped fresh chives
1/2 teaspoon (2.5 mL) fine sea salt
Pinch of cayenne pepper
8 ears of corn

Mix butter, chives, salt and cayenne together.
Set aside.
Turn barbecue to medium high heat.
Remove just a few of the outer layers of cornhusks
on each ear.
Fold back remaining husks and remove corn silk.
Spread corn kernels with chive butter and rewrap
inner husks around corn.
Grill until husks are slightly charred and corn is tender,
turning often, for about 20 minutes.
Oven method:
Put buttered corn in a preheated 350F (180C) oven.
Bake 10 to 12 minutes.
Remove from oven and serve warm.

CHAPTER
3

SERVES:
4

SEASON:
August,
September

page 77

Grower Arden Vaughn once said corn should only be eaten
the day it's picked – and she's right. Once corn is picked, the
sugars begin to convert into starch. Each day, it becomes
less sweet and more gooey. When you can find just-picked
corn, barbecuing it is the only way to go. The sugars
caramelize with the butter and the flavours are
unforgettable. Arden no longer grows corn for eating,
but raises exotic animals on her farm, Lake Land Game
Meats on the outskirts of St. Catharines.

Lake Land Game Meats,
1226 St Paul Street West, 1-800-665-3547

candied garlic on thyme roasted tomatoes

1 cup (250 mL) sugar
2 cups (500 mL) water
16 garlic cloves, peeled
1 1/2 tablespoons (22.5 mL) extra
    virgin olive oil
8 fresh roma tomatoes
Salt and freshly ground black pepper
3 tablespoons (45 mL) fresh thyme, minced
Extra virgin olive oil
16 thin slices of Italian crostini
1 raw garlic clove
6 ounces (125 grams) Niagara Gold cheese,
    room temperature

Bring water and sugar to a boil, reduce heat and add peeled garlic cloves.
Gently simmer garlic until soft, about 15 minutes.
Drain and let dry.
Warm olive oil in a skillet and sauté garlic cloves until lightly browned, stirring to coat the cloves with oil.
Slice the tomatoes in half lengthwise, scoop out and discard the seeds and pulp.
Place tomato shells on a cookie sheet, skin side down and sprinkle with salt, pepper and thyme.
Drizzle with olive oil and bake at 250F (120C) for 1 hour.
Remove from oven. Brush crostini with olive oil and rub with the raw garlic clove.
To serve, place a tomato slice on a crostini.
Top with a smearing of Niagara Gold cheese and one or two cooked garlic cloves.
Season with salt and pepper and enjoy.
Makes 16 appetizers.

CHAPTER
3

SERVES:
4 to 6

SEASON:
August,
September

page 79

Liz Black runs Goshen Farm, an organic vegetable farm in the sleepy village of Wainfleet. Liz simply wanted to feed her family better and before she knew it, she was farming. That was 20 years ago. Today, Goshen Farm grows a full range of fruit and vegetables including garlic and tomatoes, the very ingredients that make this dish so special. You can find Liz at the Grimsby Farmers Market every Thursday from 4:30 till dusk.

Goshen Farm, 33433 Sider Road, Wainfleet.

cilantro radish relish

1/2 bunch fresh cilantro
1 bunch radishes (about 5), cleaned and diced
1 spring onion, sliced finely
2 tablespoons (30 mL) honey
2 tablespoons (30 mL) white cider vinegar
1/2 jalapeno pepper, minced
Salt and freshly cracked white pepper

Pluck the cilantro leaves from the stems and wash in a salad spinner. Spin dry and place in a medium bowl.
Add diced radishes and chopped spring onion.
Toss to mix.
In a small bowl, mix honey with cider and minced jalapeno pepper.
Season to taste with salt and pepper and add to radish mixture.
Toss to completely coat.
Relish is best served within 2 hours of preparation.
Makes 1 cup.

CHAPTER
3

SERVES:
4

SEASON:
June

page 81

FARMERS' MARKETS
There are many farmers' markets in Niagara. Fonthill, Port Colborne, Grimsby and Niagara-on-the-Lake are smaller artisan markets where lots of organic and heirloom growers pile their precious produce high for the hungry shoppers. The larger markets include St Catharines and Welland and they're filled with local growers, crafters and culinary entrepreneurs who bring produce in from around the world. Either way, it's a central place where communities gather in the name of good food.

Beamsville corn confetti

4 ears barbecued corn on the cob
3 medium heirloom tomatoes, diced
1/2 red onion, diced
1/3 cup (80 mL) Ontario canola oil
1/4 cup (60 mL) verjus
1/4 cup (60 mL) fresh cilantro, minced
Salt and freshly ground black pepper
Garlic chives as garnish

Slice barbecued corn kernels off the cob into a large bowl.
Add the tomatoes and red onion and mix well.
In a small bowl, whisk together oil, lime juice and zest and pour over the corn salad, stir to coat.
Add the cilantro and season well with salt and pepper.
Let the salad sit at least 30 minutes to let the flavours develop before serving.
To serve, stir well to coat ingredients with dressing.
Garnish with fresh garlic chives.

CHAPTER

3

SERVES:
4

SEASON:
August

page 83

TO BARBECUE CORN
To barbecued corn on the cob, turn barbecue to medium high heat. Remove just a few of the outer layers of cornhusks on each ear. Fold back remaining husks and remove corn silk. Spread corn kernels with butter and rewrap inner husks around corn. Grill until husks are slightly charred and corn is tender, turning often, for about 20 minutes.

OVEN METHOD
Put buttered corn in a preheated 350F (180C) oven.
Bake 10 to 12 minutes. Remove from oven and serve warm.

Queenston frisée salad

1/4 cup (60 mL) icewine vinegar
2 teaspoons (10 mL) Kozlik's Dijon-style
   mustard
1/4 teaspoon (1 mL) dried oregano
salt and freshly ground black pepper
1/2 cup (125 mL) Ontario Canola oil
10 ounces (250 g) frisée, torn into bite-size
   pieces (8 cups)
whole grain crackers

In a large bowl, whisk together icewine vinegar, mustard, oregano, salt and pepper to taste.
Add oil in a slow stream, whisking until thick.
Toss frisée with dressing.
Divide among 4 salad plates and serve with crackers as a first course.

CHAPTER
3

SERVES:
4

SEASON:
spring

page 85

Debbie Sexsmith is nothing short of a passionate gardener. The fifth generation Sexsmith to farm the land, Debbie boards horses, raises chickens and a few rabbits, but her passion is her gardens. There are approximately 2 acres of organically grown tomatoes, beans, onions, carrots, cabbage, squash, corn, zucchini and herbs. Each year there's something different and it's likely you'll find tender baby romaine, edible herbs and flowers that make a summer salad special and on occasion, you'll find farm fresh eggs. You can buy directly from the farm on Dominion Road in Ridgeway but it's only open by chance, best to call ahead.

Sexsmith Farm, 2778 Dominion Road,
Ridgeway, 905-894-4690

distilled bruschetta

1 fresh baguette, sliced thinly on the bias
3 garlic cloves, halved
6 plum tomatoes, chopped
2 small spring onions, chopped
1/4 cup (60 mL) basil leaves, finely chopped
3 tablespoons (45 mL) Prince Igor Vodka
    from Kittling Ridge Wines & Spirits
1/2 teaspoon (2.5 mL) Billy's hot sauce
1 teaspoon freshly ground black pepper
1/2 cup (125 mL) Parmesan cheese, grated

Rub each piece of bread with garlic and place on a large cookie sheet. Bake in a 400F (200C) oven for 10 minutes or until lightly toasted. Remove from the oven and immediately sprinkle each piece with salt.
Meanwhile, mix tomatoes, onions, basil, vodka, hot sauce and black pepper in a large bowl.
Season with salt and pepper.
Mix well, cover and set aside.
To serve, spoon tomato mixture onto bread slices and top with Parmesan.

CHAPTER
3

SERVES:
4

SEASON:
August

page 87

Billy's African Hot Sauce is so darned good, it brings tears of joy to your eyes. It's a Niagara-made product created by Bilkis (aka Billy) Abdelfader, a native of Tanzania, in Eastern Africa. Hot sauces are a big part of the cuisine Billy grew up on. When she immigrated to Canada with her two children, Mohammed and Qamer, Billy made her own hot sauce because there simply wasn't any in the region to her liking. Hot sauce is all about the perfect blend of flavour and heat that doesn't overpower food but elevates it to another level of deliciousness. So Billy set out to bring her favourite cultural flavour to Niagara. She uses all Niagara-grown hot peppers and it's so delicious it won an Award of Excellence from Niagara Presents.

You can find Billy's hot sauce at Niagara Presents on Mountainview Road in Beamsville.

farmers squash with thyme

1 medium squash, try a unique variety
  from a local grower
2 tablespoons olive oil, divided
Salt and freshly ground black
2 tablespoons fresh thyme

Preheat oven to 375F (180C).
Wash the squash and cut in slices widthwise.
Scoop out the seeds from the centre and discard.
Coat with olive oil, salt and pepper to taste and place on a lined baking sheet.
Bake for approximately 30 to 35 minutes, or until well caramelized.
Remove from oven and sprinkle with thyme.
Serve warm.

CHAPTER

3

SERVES:
4

SEASON:
November,
December,
January

page 89

NIAGARA HERB FARM
A real progressive thinker, owner Arleen Mills not only supplies Niagara with many of their garden herbs, but she also grows restaurant quality vegetables and seasoning blends. Arleen specializes in lavender production, she's experimenting with northern passionfruit and she's just pickled chive blossoms for Niagara's own version of capers. You can find Arleen at many of the farmers markets. The on-farm retail shop is open weekends.

Call for times. 1177 York Road,
Niagara-on-the-Lake, 289-296-7107
www.niagaraherbfarm.com

Parmesan crusted cauliflower

1 cauliflower, washed and broken into florets
1 farm fresh egg
2 egg whites
3/4 cup (180 mL) breadcrumbs
1 teaspoon (5 mL) chopped fresh parsley
1/2 cup (125 mL) Parmesan cheese, grated
Salt and freshly ground black pepper

Place the cauliflower florets in steamer or colander
over water and steam, covered, for 10 minutes.
Allow to cool.
Meanwhile, whisk the eggs together in a bowl and
season with salt and pepper.
Place the breadcrumbs, parsley and Parmesan cheese
in a freezer bag.
Roll the cooled cauliflower in the eggs and drop in bag
with breadcrumb mixture.
Shake bag to completely cover cauliflower.
Place florets on a baking sheet and repeat until
all cauliflower is coated in breadcrumbs.
Bake in a preheated 350F (180C) oven for 20 minutes
or until browned.

CHAPTER
3

SERVES:
4

SEASON:
September,
October

page 91

Warner Orchards is a 100-acre fruit farm owned by multi-
generations of the Warner family. On the farm you can buy
just-harvested produce from strawberries, sweet cherries,
apricots, nectarines to raspberries and pumpkins. Vegetables
range from eggplant and cauliflower to zucchini and fresh corn.
You can buy right from the farm or at the Grimsby farmers
market.

Warner Orchards, 4817 Lincoln Avenue, RR#3, Beamsville.

spring onion pancakes

3 spring onions
2 large Yukon Gold potatoes
1 farm fresh egg, whisked
1 teaspoon (5 mL) salt
Freshly cracked black pepper
Ontario canola oil
1/2 cup (125 mL) sour cream
Sliced spring onion

Using the first 3 inches of the onion, slice in half lengthwise and julienne finely.
Add to a large bowl and set aside.
Scrub potatoes and pat dry. Using a mandolin, shred potato into fine matchsticks.
Working quickly, spread potatoes on a kitchen towel, roll up and press to remove as much moisture from the potatoes as possible.
Add potatoes to onions with whisked egg.
Season with salt and pepper and mix until onion and potatoes are coated in egg.
Add canola to a large skillet to approximately 1/2-inch depth and heat over medium high heat.
Using kitchen tongs, drop mounds of potato mixture into the hot oil, careful not to have them touch each other.
Flatten lightly to make a pancake.
Cook for approximately 3 minutes, until browned on bottom, then carefully turn over to brown the top.
Remove from the oil with a slotted spoon and drain on paper towels.
Repeat until all potato pancake mixture is used.
Serve warm with sour cream on the side and garnish with sliced spring onions.

CHAPTER
3

SERVES:
4

SEASON:
May, June

page 93

Trembling Aspen Herb Farm is a 10-acre organic farm in Caistor Centre run by Ed and Susan Dolan. Ed is a passionate farmer who's been involved with organics since its inception. Their main product is herbs from which they make flavoured oils, vinegars, spice mixes and herb jellies and they also grow a variety of organic vegetables to sell at the Grimsby Farmers Market and on their farm.

Trembling Aspen Herb Farm, 9689 Concession 3, Caistor Centre.

panfried Niagara Gold and hazelnut salad

1/4 cup (60 mL) Grimo hazelnuts
4 tablespoons (60 mL) hazelnut oil from
    Grimo Nut Nursery
1 teaspoon (5 mL) Dijon-style mustard
2 tablespoons (30 mL) Aceto Niagara
    Icewine vinegar
Salt and freshly cracked black pepper
6 cups (1.5 L) Bibb lettuce
All-purpose flour for dusting
3 tablespoons (45 mL) Ontario canola oil
4 slices Niagara Gold cheese, 1/4-inch thick

In a small skillet over medium heat, toast the hazelnuts
until golden, about 5 minutes.
Let cool and chop.
Set aside.
In a small glass jar with lid, combine hazelnut oil, mustard,
vinegar, half the toasted hazelnuts, salt and pepper.
Shake well.
Pour over lettuce and toss. Divide between 4 salad plates.
Heat canola oil in skillet until hot.
Dredge the cheese in flour to coat both sides and
place in skillet.
Cook, turning once, until golden on both sides,
3 to 4 minutes.
Lay a slice of cheese on top of each salad, sprinkle
evenly with remaining nuts and serve warm.

CHAPTER

3

SERVES:
4

SEASON:
summer

SERVE WITH:
Tawse Winery
Sketches of
Niagara Unoaked
Chardonnay,
www.
tawsewinery.ca

Wolfgang Woerthle operates a 100-acre grape farm in
Niagara-on-the-Lake and Martin Gemmrich is a winemaker.
The two men teamed up to produce a line of vinegars and
vinegar-based aperitifs called Aceto Niagara. Woerthle and
Gemmrich grow as much of their own fruit as they can,
affording them control over the harvest. What they don't
grow, such as sour cherries or tomatoes, they buy locally,
working with local farmers to oversee high levels of
quality. Although, icewine vinegar is their signature
product, they also produce a line of fruit vinegars
such as sour cherry, peach, apricot, and tomato
vinegar. No short cuts are taken, no flavourings,
preservatives or additives are used.

Aceto Niagara
www.acetoniagara.com

market square zucchini au gratin

1 teaspoon (10 mL) butter
2 teaspoon (5 mL) Ontario canola oil
1 white onion, peeled and minced
4 zucchini
10 slices prosciutto
1/2 cup (125 mL) fine breadcrumbs
2 teaspoons (10 mL) fresh rosemary
1/4 cup (60 mL) Parmesan cheese,
    freshly grated
2 tablespoons (30 mL) extra virgin olive oil

Heat the butter and oil in a skillet over medium heat.
Add onion and cook until soft, about 3 minutes.
Transfer to a 9-inch baking dish.
Cut off the ends of the zucchini, and slice lengthwise about 1/4-inch thick.
Place a half slice of prosciutto on top of each zucchini slice.
Layer the zucchini and prosciutto over the onions, slightly overlapping.
Season to taste.
Put the breadcrumbs, rosemary and Parmesan cheese into a food processor.
Pulse until well incorporated.
Sprinkle breadcrumb mixture over the zucchini and drizzle with oil.
Bake at 325F (160C) for 25 minutes.
Serve warm.

CHAPTER
3

SERVES:
4

SEASON:
July,
August

page 97

Zucchini is the quintessential Italian summer vegetable.
Anyone who's ever grown zucchini in a backyard garden knows it proliferates unbelievably. I say thank goodness because the most incredible experience is zucchini flowers sautéed with herbs and Niagara sparkling wine. Young and tender zucchini are an exciting vegetable that carry the flavours of whatever you pair them with from pasta sauces to main courses.
Be picky and insist on the smaller zucchini for a sweeter flavour and be careful, you just might start a love affair with zucchini.

green garden salad

2 tablespoons (30 mL) extra-virgin olive oil
1 tablespoon (15 mL) Niagara Verjus
1 tablespoon (15 mL) minced shallots
6 cups (1.5 mL) rinsed garden lettuce
Salt and freshly ground black pepper

In a large bowl, whisk together olive oil, verjus
and minced shallot.
Add salt and pepper to taste.
Add garden greens and gently toss.

CHAPTER
3

SERVES:
4

SEASON:
April, May,
June

page 99

Verjuice literally means 'green juice'. It's made from pressing unripe grapes so the acidity remains relatively high. A tart, acidic condiment such as this is often used as a culinary alternative to lemon juice or vinegar. It was once a traditional kitchen staple in Europe but was forsaken for wine in cooking and flavoured vinegars in salads. It still is very popular in France and Australia but is not widely known in Niagara. Crown Bench Estate Winery sells a delicious verjus and Featherstone Estate Winery not only sells it but whips it up into a Niagara version of lemonade for a thirst quenching drink on a hot Niagara day.

The produce of Niagara is secured by innovative chefs
who create a world-class culinary collaboration
that depends as much on the production of its ingredients
as it does on the transformation of
those ingredients into a delicious dish.

farm raised meat and poultry

CHAPTER **4**

page 101

sweet garlic chicken

2 tablespoons (30 mL) unsalted butter
1 tablespoon (15 mL) Ontario canola oil
4 chicken breasts
24 garlic cloves, unpeeled
3 ounces (75 g) white button mushrooms, coarsely chopped
1/4 cup (60 mL) dry white wine
1 cup (250 mL) chicken broth
Salt and freshly ground black pepper
1 teaspoon (5 mL) minced parsley

Preheat oven to 450F (220C).
In a large oven-proof skillet, heat butter and oil over moderately high heat. Sauté chicken breasts, turning until lightly browned on both sides, about 5 minutes.
Scatter the garlic cloves around the chicken.
Place the skillet in the oven and roast until the chicken juices run clear, about 20 to 25 minutes.
Remove chicken from the skillet and tent with aluminum foil to keep warm.
Add mushrooms to the skillet and sauté over moderately high heat until browned, about 2 minutes.
Add the wine and scrape up any browned bits from the bottom of the skillet.
Cook until reduced by half, about 5 minutes.
Transfer the garlic, mushrooms and liquid to a blender and purée.
In a small saucepan, bring the broth to a boil.
Reduce the heat to low and stir in the garlic and mushroom purée.
Season with salt and pepper and remove from the heat.
Place the chicken on a warmed serving platter.
Spoon the sauce overtop and sprinkle with the parsley.
Serve the remaining sauce separately.

CHAPTER
4

SERVES:
4

SEASON:
December, January, February

SERVE WITH:
Coyote's Run Estate Winery Unoaked Chardonnay, www. coyotesrunwinery. com

Maureen and Doug MacSween run Quiet Acres Farm and a bustling little market stand on the intersection of Lakeshore Road and East West Line in Niagara-on-the-Lake that is anything but quiet. This could very well be Niagara's garlic central. They start with garlic scapes in the spring and harvest elephant garlic by the end of June - always selling out by mid-August. Their garlic is pulled daily and if you ever thought elephant garlic was milder garlic then you've never had it fresh. It's ultra sweet in a garlicky sort of way – delicious!

The market stand is open seasonally and you can also find them at the Niagara-on-the-Lake Farmers Market.

crown roast pork with smoked sausage and apple stuffing

7-pound (3.18 kg) crown roast of pork
   prepared by butcher
1 pound smoked Good Shepherd pork sausage
2 tablespoons (30 mL) unsalted butter
1 large onion, diced
3 cloves garlic, minced
2 stalks celery, diced
1 teaspoon (5 mL) dried thyme leaves
1 teaspoon (5 mL) dried sage leaves
3 medium Northern Spy apples, cored, sliced
3 slices day-old bread, cubed

Preheat oven to 450F (230C).
Lay crown roast upside-down on a rack in roasting pan.
Place in oven and immediately turn oven down to 350F (180C). Cook for 1 1/2 hours.
Meanwhile, remove the sausage from its casing.
In a large skillet set over medium-high heat melt half the butter and add sausage meat.
Break up sausage and sauté until lightly browned and cooked through.
Transfer sausage meat to paper towels to drain.
In the same pan melt remaining butter and sauté onions with the garlic, celery, thyme and sage until onions are translucent and celery is crisp tender.
Add apples and sauté for one minute more.
Remove from heat.
Transfer to a large bowl and add cubed bread, mix well and set aside.
When roast is ready, remove from oven.
Turn roast upright with bones forming a crown and pile stuffing in crown.
Return to oven and bake for an additional hour.
Remove from oven and let sit for 10 minutes.

SERVES:
8

SEASON:
December,
January,
February

SERVE WITH:
Marynissen Estates
Winery Cabernet/
Merlot,
www.marynissen.
com.

page 105

The Good Shepherd is a little farm store that represents family community living. Six Mennonite families in all raise cattle, pigs and chicken in a natural environment. The family-trained butchers then prepare the various cuts of meat and offer some convenience products such as breaded chicken, stuffed chicken breasts and turkey burgers. As well as meat, the families make their own cheese, smoked products and delicious summer sausage. During the summer their organic garden thrives with fresh vegetables that are picked when you arrive or can be purchased from the chilled room adjacent the store. Visiting the Good Shepherd is an experience in country life and community values.

The Good Shepherd, 3922 Younge Street, Vineland.

grilled duck breasts with icewined apricots

4 duck breasts
1 tablespoon (15 mL) Niagara honey
8 dried apricots
4 tablespoons (60 mL) Vidal icewine
1 tablespoon (15 mL) unsalted butter
3 tablespoons (45 mL) Ontario canola oil
2 tablespoons (30 mL) unsalted butter
Salt and freshly cracked black pepper
Thyme sprigs for garnish

Brush the duck breasts with honey and sprinkle with
a little salt.
Set aside.
Place apricots and icewine in a bowl and set aside to soak.
Preheat oven to 350F (180C).
Warm an oven-proof skillet over medium high heat and
add butter and oil.
Score the fat side of the duck breasts and lay,
skin-side down, in skillet.
Brown on both sides, about 4 minutes per side.
Season with salt and pepper and transfer to oven to finish
off, approximately 6 minutes.
Meanwhile, melt butter in small skillet over medium
heat and add icewine-soaked apricots with juices.
Cook for 3 to 4 minutes or until warmed through.
Remove duck from oven and let sit for 5 minutes.
To serve, lay a duck breast on each of 4 dinner plates
and top with warm apricots and icewine glaze.

SERVES:
4

SEASON:
January,
February,
March

SERVE WITH:
Mountain Road
Wine Company
Red,
www.
mountainroadwine.
com

Since 1995 Bill and Arden Vaughn of Lake Land Game Meats
in St Catharines have sold exotic meats from their 250-acre
farm. They raise red deer, wild boar and beef cattle (a
delicious cross between Hereford and Angus) on their farm.
You'll see a few horses pasturing as well, but they're just
for fun. What the Vaughns don't raise, they source from
the very best farms they can find and they stay as local as
possible; duck breast, fresh quail eggs, salt and pepper elk
sausage, venison burgers or pepperettes, bison jerky,
wild boar sausage.

Lake Land Game Meats, 1226 St. Paul Street West,
St. Catharines 905-688-4570

farmers sausage with tri-coloured peppers

6 fresh Italian sausage links, hot or mild
2 tablespoons (30 mL) Ontario canola oil
1 large red bell pepper, seeded and sliced
1 large yellow bell pepper, seeded and sliced
1 large green bell pepper, seeded and sliced
1 onion, peeled and sliced
1 clove garlic, minced
1 teaspoon (5 mL) dried thyme leaves

Slice the sausage into thin pieces.
Warm 1 tablespoon of canola oil in a skillet and add sausage.
Cook over medium heat until sausage is completely cooked, about 8 minutes, shaking the skillet to move the sausage around.
Remove from pan.
Add the other teaspoon of canola oil to the skillet then add the peppers and onion.
Cook for 4 to 5 minutes, or until onion is soft and translucent.
Add the garlic, thyme leaves and cooked sausage.
Cook for another minute or two, stirring to combine the flavours.

CHAPTER
4

SERVES:
4

SEASON:
August, September

SERVE WITH:
Lakeview Cellars Baco Noir Reserve, www. lakeviewcellars. on.ca

page 109

It's an amazing 42-acres under glass with an additional 18-acres currently underway. This is St. Davids Hydroponics, a gigantic greenhouse facility that grows peppers – red, yellow, and orange bell peppers. The state of the art operation is completely environmentally friendly, and natural plant food and management techniques replace the need for chemical pesticides or fertilizers. Your can get St. Davids produce at Pairings Specialty Food Market in Niagara-on-the-Lake.

Don't miss the Ontario Sausage Festival in July at Lipa Park in Fonthill
www.stcatharines.ca/tourism/festivals_events_summer.asp

fennel crusted rack of pork

1 small fennel with 2 inches of fronds
attached, coarsely chopped
1 onion, coarsely chopped
6 cloves garlic, peeled and sliced
2 teaspoons (10 mL) fresh thyme,
finely chopped
2 teaspoons (10 mL) fresh sage,
finely chopped
2 teaspoons (10 mL) fresh oregano,
finely chopped
2 teaspoons (10 mL) fennel seeds
1 1/2 teaspoons (7.5 mL) coarsely ground
white pepper
1 4 1/2-pound pork rib roast, Frenched
by your butcher
Coarse salt

In a food processor fitted with the metal blade, combine
the fennel and fennel fronds, onion and garlic and
process to a paste.
Add the thyme, sage, oregano, fennel seeds and
pepper and pulse to combine.
With a small, sharp knife, make shallow crosshatch
cuts in the fat layer of the pork roast.
Season it all over with salt, rubbing it in well.
Rub the fennel-garlic paste over the roast to cover it with a
layer about 1/4 inch thick.
Cover and refrigerate for at least 1 hour and up to 8 hours.
Preheat the oven to 350F (180C).
About 20 minutes before cooking, remove the roast from
the refrigerator and let it sit at room temperature.
Transfer the pork to a roasting pan and roast for
about 1 hour and 15 minutes.
Remove the roast from the oven and cover it loosely
with foil. Let it rest for 15 to 20 minutes before slicing it
into thick chops.

CHAPTER
4

SERVES:
6

SEASON:
August,
September

SERVE WITH:
Niagara College
Teaching Winery
Pinot Noir,
www.
nctwinery.ca

page 111

In 2002, Niagara College launched Canada's first teaching
winery at the Niagara-on-the-Lake campus. The Niagara
College Winery and Viticulture Program trains students in
vineyard management and practical winemaking skills.
The students all have a hand in making the wine under the
guidance of veteran winemaker Terrence VanRooyen. The
wine is spectacular, is raved about by the wine press, wins
countless medals and the small quantities sold through
their on-campus retail store have earned them a loyal
following. Proceeds from wine sales go directly back into
the program to maintain its status as Canada's leading,
practical, hands-on, wine training facility, www.nctwinery.ca

grilled lamb burgers with cucumber yogurt

1 pound (450 g) ground lamb
1 small onion, finely minced
1 farm fresh egg
1/2 cup (125 mL) seasoned breadcrumbs
1 teaspoon (5 mL) ground cumin
Salt and freshly cracked black pepper
4 whole grain hamburger rolls

Mix lamb with onion, egg, breadcrumbs and cumin.
Season with salt and pepper and form into 4 large patties.
Heat a grill to high and grill the patties for
6 minutes per side.
Serve on rolls with cucumber yogurt.

CHAPTER

4

SERVES:
4

SEASON:
summer

SERVE WITH:
Calamus Estate
Winery Red,
www.
calamuswinery.
com

cucumber yogurt

1/2 English cucumber, peeled, seeded, and grated
1/2 cup (125 mL) plain whole milk yogurt
2 teaspoons (10 mL) fresh verjus
2 teaspoons (10 mL) chopped fresh mint
1 small garlic clove, minced
Salt and freshly cracked black pepper

Mix all ingredients together and chill.
Serve on or with lamb burgers.

Liz Black simply wanted to feed her family healthy food and before she knew it, she was farming. That was 20 years ago. Today, Goshen Farm raises lamb as natural as possible. The first two months the lambs are fed by their mother, when they are old enough to eat, crushed grains, hay and pasture grass are introduced to their diet. The lamb roam free, grow slower, eat naturally their whole lives and are drug free.

You can find Liz at the Port Colborne, Ridgeway and Grimsby Farmers Markets, or buy direct from Goshen Farm, 33433 Sider Road, Wainfleet.

Craig's honeyed ham

1 country-cured ham
2 bay leaves
1 onion, peeled and stuck with 2 cloves
3 cups (750 mL) off-dry Riesling
3 tablespoons (45 mL) brown sugar
1 teaspoon (5 mL) ground cinnamon
1/2 teaspoon (2.5 mL) ground nutmeg
2 tablespoons (30 mL) Niagara honey
Whole cloves

Soak the ham for 24 to 30 hours in cold water to cover.
Drain. Place in a kettle or roasting dish with close fitting
lid. Tuck the bay leaves around the ham, add the onion,
Riesling and enough water to cover.
Bring to a boil, cover and simmer very gently for 2 1/2
hours or until large bone in heavy end of ham becomes
loose and protrudes.
Lift the ham from the stock and place in a roasting pan
to cool. Mix the brown sugar, cinnamon, nutmeg and
honey to form a paste.
As soon as the ham is cool enough to handle, remove
the skin and with a sharp knife, make diagonal cuts
1/8-inch deep and 3/4-inch apart in the fat layer to
make a diamond pattern.
Rub in the honey paste and stud with cloves.
Preheat the oven to 375F (190C).
Pour the cooking stock around the ham in the roasting
pan to a depth of 1/2-inch.
Bake, basting occasionally for 20 to 30 minutes or
until the coating looks crisp and golden.
Serve hot or cold, sliced thinly with seasonal vegetables.

CHAPTER
4

SERVES:
8 to 10

SEASON:
February,
March,
April

SERVE WITH:
Megalomaniac
Pink Slip Rose,
www.
megalomaniacwine.
com.

page 115

Honeys are very diverse and flavourful, more so than most
people think. They can be light and delicate, dark, deep and
nutty, intensely perfumed and more – each varietal honey is
distinctively different from the next. Charlie Bee Honey is
the region's largest honey producer by Niagara standards,
but small in the world of honey. Charlie manages over 5,900
beehives, producing many different honeys from an elegant
blueberry honey to a hearty buckwheat.

Charlie Bee Honey, 3591 Mountain Road,
Beamsville 905-563-7285

gourmet settings

marinated picnic steak

1 pound (450 g) flank steak
3 tablespoons (45 mL) soy sauce
2 tablespoons (30 mL) lemon juice
2 tablespoons (30 mL) Ontario canola oil
1 tablespoon (15 mL) brown sugar
1 garlic clove, crushed
Freshly cracked black pepper

Put the steak in a shallow dish just large enough to hold it snugly.
Whisk remaining ingredients together and pour over steak.
Cover and marinate for 1 to 2 hours.
Place on a broiler pan and broil for 6 to 8 minutes per side.
Remove from oven and let rest for 10 minutes.
Slice diagonally and serve warm with simple salad.

CHAPTER
4

SERVES:
4

SEASON:
August,
September,
October

SERVE WITH:
Thirty Bench
Benchmark
Red, www.
thirtybench.com

Gryphon Ridge Highlands is a small 10-acre cattle farm in Niagara-on-the-Lake, owned by Kim McQuhae. Kim's love of animals led her to become a cattle rancher. Highland cattle are stocky looking cows with long hair and curled horns. Because of their long hair, Highland cattle don't accumulate the top layer of body fat like traditional cattle, so the meat is naturally leaner with very fine marbling throughout. They're naturally raised – no hormones or steroids. The meat is aged anywhere from 21 to 28 days for added tenderness and increased flavour. "This is how steak used to taste," declares Kim.

Gryphon Ridge Highlands, 1324 Larkin Road,
Niagara on the Lake, 905-468-5603

crusted chicken

24 saltine crackers
4 whole chicken legs
1/4 cup (60 mL) unsalted butter, melted
1/2 cup (125 mL) grated Parmesan cheese
1 teaspoon (5 mL) freshly ground black pepper
1/2 cup (125 mL) balsamic vinegar from
   Niagara Vinegars

Preheat oven to 300F (150C).
Pulse crackers in a food processor until they resemble fine crumbs.
Spread the crumbs on a baking sheet and bake until crumbs are dry but not toasted, about 6 to 8 minutes.
Shake the sheet twice during baking.
Be careful not to let the crumbs brown.
Remove from oven and allow to cool.
Raise oven temperature to 325F (165C).
Brush chicken legs generously with butter.
Pour toasted cracker crumbs, Parmesan and black pepper into a large resealable plastic bag.
Add chicken, seal the bag and shake to coat chicken.
Place in a baking dish that has been sprayed with a non-stick oil and bake for 1 hour or until golden brown.
Serve balsamic vinegar on the side for dunking.

CHAPTER
4

SERVES:
4

SEASON:
all year

SERVE WITH:
Chateau des
Charmes
Auxerrois,
www.
chateaudescharmes.
com

page 119

The Paron family has been making Parmesan cheese for over 76 years. It started when Louie Paron immigrated to Canada in 1930 from Italy and brought with him his skill and love of cheese. Today Paron Cheese Company produces an incredibly delicious Parmesan and Montasio cheese in a natural and traditional way. It's available at their retail store on Highway 20, but Mrs. Paron wants everyone to know it's the cheese shop at the back of the road and not the one in front.

Paron Cheese Co., 400 Hwy 20 East, RR #1, Hannon, Ontario

pork medallions in merlot reduction

2 tablespoons (30 mL) unsalted butter
2 tablespoons (30 mL) Ontario canola oil
1 pork tenderloin
2 onions, sliced into rings
1 teaspoon (5 mL) thyme, dried
1/2 cup (125 mL) beef broth
1/2 cup (125 mL) Merlot
1 1/2 teaspoons (7.5 mL) dried tarragon, crumbled
1 tablespoon (15 mL) Dijon-style mustard
Salt and freshly ground black pepper

In large skillet, heat butter and oil over medium high heat.
Season pork all over with salt and pepper and sauté 5 to 8 minutes per side.
Remove from skillet and keep warm.
Add onions and thyme, reduce heat to medium.
Cook until onions are wilted, about 5 minutes.
Season with salt and pepper. Remove from skillet and keep warm.
Add broth, Merlot and tarragon.
Cook until reduced to about 1/4 cup, about 10 minutes.
Whisk in mustard and season with salt and pepper.
Return pork to pan and heat gently.
Cook for 5 minutes.
Meanwhile divide the onions on 4 dinner plates.
Cut pork into 8 slices and place 2 slices on onions.
Drizzle with Merlot reduction sauce and serve warm.

CHAPTER
4

SERVES:
4

SEASON:
December, January, February

SERVE WITH:
Stratus Vineyards Red, www. straturswines.com

NIAGARA PRODUCE
The produce of Niagara is special. It's grown on the same soils and enjoys the same climatic and geographical influences that make our wine grapes so special. Yet, many people take for granted the wealth of ingredients and quality of these ingredients available in Niagara and are maybe only vaguely conscious of the groundswell - now amounting to an unstoppable movement – of Niagara artisan farmers turning out some of the finest foodstuffs currently being produced in this country. How lucky are the folks of Niagara to be so connected to their food source.

potted chicken

6 chicken legs
2 tablespoon (30 mL) Ontario canola oil
Salt and pepper
2 tablespoons (30 mL) unsalted butter
1 large onion, diced
3 carrots, thinly sliced
3 celery stalks, thinly sliced
1/2 cup (125 mL) all-purpose flour
2 1/2 cups (675 mL) chicken stock
1 1/2 cups (375 mL) whole milk
1 teaspoon (5 mL) chopped fresh thyme leaves
1/4 cup (60 mL) dry sherry
3/4 cup (180 m) fresh green peas
2 tablespoons (30 mL) minced fresh parsley
Salt and freshly ground black pepper

In a medium skillet, heat canola oil to medium high heat.
Add chicken legs and cook until browned on all sides,
about 6 minutes.
Remove from skillet, season with salt and pepper
and set aside.
In a large skillet, melt butter on medium heat.
Add the onions, carrots and celery, and cook until the
onions are translucent, about 10 minutes.
Add the flour and cook, stirring, one minute more.
Whisk in chicken stock and milk.
Decrease the heat to low and simmer for 10 minutes,
stirring often.
Meanwhile, preheat oven to 400F (200C).
Add the thyme, sherry, peas, parsley, salt and pepper
to the vegetables and stir well.
Taste and adjust seasoning if necessary.
Place 1 chicken leg inverted (knuckle side down) in
each of 6 10-ounce ramekins, and top with vegetables.
Bake for 25 minutes, or until the filling is bubbling.
Let cool for at least 5 minutes before serving.

CHAPTER

4

SERVES:
6

SEASON:
November,
December

SERVE WITH:
Henry of Pelham
Winery
Pinot Blanc,
www.
henryofpelham
winery.com

Cheryl and Barney Barnes run an 8-acre farm on Seventh
Street Louth on the brimming edge of St. Catharines. Inn
the Pines is the incredibly busy fruit stand on the property
right in front of the market garden in full view of
customers, reminding them where their fresh vegetables
are coming from. If Cheryl happens to run out of
something, she just picks it fresh for you. Rows of salad
greens and vegetables are grown in strip beds and crops
are rotated so they don't have to be sprayed. The
vegetables and herbs are delicious and grown naturally,
a perfect accompaniment for this chicken dish. Cheryl sells
her produce from her busy stand along with fresh eggs
from the 60 laying hens she raises.

Inn the Pines, 1320 Seventh Street Louth, St. Catharines.

prime rib roast with cabernet au jus

6 cups (1.5 L) (2-750 mL bottles)
   Cabernet Franc
4 cups (1 L) beef stock
2 cups (500 mL) ruby port
3 large garlic cloves, peeled
1 large shallot, peeled, halved
2 bay leaves
1 teaspoon (5 mL) dried thyme
1 6-pound (2.72 kg) prime rib beef roast
4 large garlic cloves, cut in half
2 teaspoons (10 mL) dried thyme
Salt and freshly ground black pepper

The day before, combine the wine, stock, port, 3 cloves garlic, shallot, bay leaves and thyme in a large saucepan.
Boil until reduced to 2 cups, about 1 hour.
Cool, cover and refrigerate.
Preheat oven to 550F (280C).
Place the roast, fat side up, on a rack in a heavy roasting pan. Rub beef all over with cut garlic cloves and 2 teaspoons thyme and season generously with salt and pepper.
Reduce heat immediately to 350F (180C) and cook for 18 to 20 minutes per pound for medium rare.
Remove from oven and let stand 20 minutes.
Separate fat from pan juices in the roasting pan.
Place pan over medium-high heat.
Add Cabernet mixture to pan and bring to boil, scraping up any browned bits.
Season to taste with salt and pepper.
Pour jus into sauceboat.
Carve beef and serve with roasted potatoes, passing jus separately.

NOTE:
To cook evenly, the roast must be at room temperature. Let it stand for 3 hours. If the roast is not at room temperature, it will take longer to cook and won't cook evenly.

CHAPTER
4

SERVES:
6 to 8

SEASON:
December,
January,
February

SERVE WITH:
Frog Pond Farm
Organic Cabernet
Franc,
www.
frogpondfarm.ca

page 125

Hommer's Meats is an artisan abattoir serving up plenty of fresh lamb, beef, pork and chicken from their retail store on Point Abino Road in Stevensville. When you drive up the long stone driveway the age-worn block building in front of you is not a pretty picture. But Hommer's customers don't complain, they just boast about the quality and flavour. The long meat counter is stacked with extra thick cuts of beef and pork, a bit of lamb, and piles of chicken. All of Hommer's meat is drug-free and air chilled. The cattle come from a wide area of Southern Ontario. Wow, it's a visual feast sure to ignite any barbecuer's appetite.

Hommer's Meats, 2909 Point Abino Road North, Stevensville, ON L0S 1S0, 905-382-2629

rosemary rack of lamb

1 large garlic clove, peeled
3 tablespoons (45 mL) chopped fresh rosemary
3 tablespoons (45 mL) chopped fresh thyme
3 tablespoons (45 mL) chopped fresh parsley
1/3 cup (80 mL) Parmesan cheese,
    finely grated
5 teaspoons (25 mL) Dijon-style mustard
Salt and freshly cracked black pepper
1 rack of Ontario lamb,
    trimmed by your butcher

Mince garlic and herbs in a food processor.
Add cheese and process just until mixture is blended.
Preheat oven to 425F (220C).
Season lamb generously with salt and pepper and
rub with mustard.
Arrange, bone side down, on a baking rack in a
small baking pan.
Press herb/cheese mixture onto mustard, coating lamb
completely. Roast approximately 30 to 40 minutes.
Remove from oven and let lamb rest 15 minutes.
Transfer lamb to cutting board.
Cut between bones into individual or double chops.
Divide between 2 plates and serve warm.

CHAPTER

4

SERVES:
2

SEASON:
January,
February,
March

SERVE WITH:
Mike Weir
Estate Winery
2005 Cabernet
Shiraz,
www.
weirwines.com

In 2007, Featherstone Estate Winery owners Dave Johnson and Louise Engel purchased 5 lambs for their vineyard. Dave, with his New Zealand sensibilities purchased the lambs to do the job of vineyard leaf plucking. Being constant eaters, the lambs ate the grape leaves all around the grapes, yet left the bitter unripened grapes to hang on the vine. The result was full sun exposure around the berries, allowing them to ripen fully. It's a brilliant piece of environmentally friendly vineyard management and delicious, vinously flavoured lamb.

www.featherstonewinery.com

roasted blonde ale chicken

1 1/2 cups (375 mL) Niagara's Best Blonde
    Premium Ale
1 cup (250 mL) apple cider
1 teaspoon (5 mL) whole peppercorns
6 whole allspice berries
2 fresh bay leaves
1/4 cup (60 mL) Ontario canola oil
1 12-pound (5.4 kg) roasting chicken
1/4 cup (60 mL) maple syrup
1/4 cup (60 mL) dried cranberries

Combine ale and cider, spices and oil in large saucepan and bring to a simmer.
Remove from heat and let cool 10 to 15 minutes.
Wash and rinse outside and cavity of chicken.
Place in food-grade plastic bucket and pour marinade over it. Add enough water to cover the chicken.
Cover with plastic wrap and refrigerate overnight.
After 12 hours, remove bird from marinade and pour marinade through sieve into 1-gallon stockpot.
Bring to boil, skim off foam and reduce heat to simmer. Simmer for 10 minutes.
Put 1 cup (250 mL) of marinade into a blender with maple syrup and dried cranberries.
Hold blender lid on top with towel, and purée until cranberries are well minced.
Place bird in roasting pan and roast at 350F (180C) for 2 1/2 hours, basting often with cranberry cider ale marinade, mixed with pan drippings.
Let chicken rest 20 to 30 minutes before carving.

CHAPTER
4

SERVES:
6

SEASON:
all year

SERVE WITH:
Niagara's Best Blonde Premium Ale

page 129

Thiessen Farms is a 17-acre farm that produces so many different fruits and vegetables you'd think it was five times the size. Owners Ron and Lorie Thiessen, along with their daughter Amy, grow everything from Asian vegetables to edamame beans. Ron's favourite vegetables are tomatoes so he grows more than 50 different kinds of tomatoes from heirloom to cherry. When it comes to squash, they grow everything weird and wonderful all colours, all shapes and all sizes.

Look for Thiessen Farms at the Grimsby Farmers' Market or shop at the farm, 4132 15th Street, Jordan Station.

rolled leg of lamb

6 garlic cloves
2 sprigs fresh rosemary, destemmed
2 tablespoons (30 mL) extra virgin olive oil
Salt and freshly cracked black pepper
1 7-pound (3.18 kg) leg of lamb,
   deboned by butcher
1/2 cup (125 mL) dry red wine or beef broth

In a food processor, purée garlic, rosemary, olive oil, salt and pepper.
Untie lamb and spread flat.
Spread most of the garlic/rosemary purée all over the lamb.
Roll up and tie tightly with butcher's twine.
Spread the remaining purée over lamb.
Lay on a rack in roasting pan and let stand at room temperature for 30 minutes. Preheat oven to 450F (220C).
Place in oven and immediately reduce heat to 350F (180C).
Roast lamb in middle of oven for 2 hours for medium rare.
Transfer to a cutting board and let stand 5 to 10 minutes.
Meanwhile, add wine to pan and deglaze by boiling over moderately high heat, stirring and scraping up brown bits, about 1 minute.
Season pan juices with salt and pepper and serve with lamb.

SERVES:
4

SEASON:
December,
January,
February

SERVE WITH:
Creekside Estate
Winery Broken
Press Shiraz,
www.
creeksideestate
winery.com

page 131

Michelle Seaborn of Silmaril Farm raises sheep. Dorset, Hampshire and Texel are just a few of the tasty breeds raised for meat production while Merino is raised for its fine wool. Lambs are fed a natural grain-based diet with hay. In the spring the animals are moved to pasture during the day and receive a grain ration in the barn at night. Michelle breed's lamb in the spring, summer and early fall, to provide fresh and frozen lamb from Easter until Christmas. The second Sunday of May they host a free annual Fleece and Fibrefest event. It's a fun afternoon for the entire family. There are farm animals to discover, sheep shearing to watch and plenty of just cooked lamb to eat. Michelle can be found at the Grimsby farmers' market.

Silmaril Farm, 144 Russ Road, Grimsby.
Farm stand open by chance.

sage veal roast

1 5-pound (2.27 kg) boneless veal roast
2 onions, minced
1 cup (250 mL) minced celery
3 tablespoons (45 mL) butter
1/2 cup (125 mL) minced parsley
1 tablespoon (15 mL) chopped fresh sage
1 clove garlic, minced
1/2 cup (125 mL) Parmesan cheese, grated
1/2 cup (125 mL) breadcrumbs
Salt and freshly ground black pepper
Whole sage leaves for garnish

Preheat oven to 350F (160C).
Cut horizontally through the centre of the veal roast creating a large slit for stuffing.
Sauté onions and celery in butter for 5 minutes.
Stir in parsley, sage and garlic. Remove from heat, add cheese and breadcrumbs and season to taste.
Open the slit in the veal roast with your fingers and stuff with onion mixture.
Lightly pepper the veal and overlap sage leaves on top.
Roast 1 1/2 hours.

CHAPTER
4

SERVES:
8

SEASON:
all year

SERVE WITH:
Ridgepoint
Wines
Nebbiolo,
www.
ridgepointwines.
com

page 133

Houweling Greenhouses in St. Anne's is a 4,000 square foot greenhouse with an additional 4,000 square foot area of production outside. Here the Houweling family, Renee, Ray and their 5 children produce incredible perennials as well as orange, yellow and red mini and large tomatoes, mini green peppers and herbs. The Houwelings sell herbs individually and also in mixed baskets, perfect for patio and balconies.

You'll find them at the Grimsby Farmers Market or at their greenhouse – but call first, there is no retail store on the property, 905-562-3321

vineyard cabernet capon

24 pearl onions
4 strips lean bacon, cut into 1-inch pieces
4 tablespoons (60 mL) unsalted butter
1 whole capon, from Kent Heritage Farms,
    cut into quarters
2 tablespoons (30 mL) all-purpose flour
1/4 cup (60 mL) Ontario brandy, Kittling Ridge
3 cups (750 mL) Cabernet Franc
8 whole cloves garlic
6 fresh thyme sprigs
4 fresh parsley sprigs
2 dried bay leaves
Salt and freshly ground black pepper
2 pounds (.91 kg) white mushrooms,
    brushed clean

In a saucepan, cover the pearl onions with water and simmer for 10 minutes. Drain, cut off the root ends and slip off the skins. Set aside. In a skillet over medium high heat, sauté bacon until crisp. Set aside. In a deep, heavy pan with a lid, melt half the butter over medium heat. When it foams, reduce heat to medium-low, add the bacon and onions and cook stirring for about 4 minutes. Using a slotted spoon, transfer the bacon and onions to a plate. Add the capon to the pot and raise the heat to medium. Cook, turning as you need, until the capon browns on both sides, about 10 minutes. Sprinkle with flour and turn from time to time until the capon and the flour are browned, about 5 minutes. Pour brandy over the capon and cook for 2 minutes. Remove capon from pan. Pour in a little of the wine and deglaze the pan, stirring to dislodge any bits clinging to the bottom. Pour in the remaining wine and return the capon, bacon and onions to the pan. Bring to a simmer and add the garlic, thyme, parsley, bay leaves, pepper and salt.
Cover and simmer, stirring occasionally until the capon is cooked through, about 45 to 50 minutes.
Meanwhile in a skillet over medium-high heat, melt the remaining butter. When it foams, add the mushrooms and sauté until lightly golden, 3 to 4 minutes.
Remove from the heat and set aside.
About 15 minutes before the capon is done, add the mushrooms. When the capon is finished cooking, using a slotted spoon transfer the capon, onions, mushrooms and bacon to a bowl. Discard the herb sprigs. Raise the heat to high and boil until the liquid is reduced by nearly half, about 5 minutes.
Return the capon, onions and mushrooms to the pan. Reduce the heat to low and cook, stirring until heated through, 3 to 4 minutes. To serve, place a piece of capon on a dish and surround with mushrooms and onions.

When it comes to artisan chicken, the locals will tell you Paul Kent is your man. Owner of Kent Heritage Farm in the village of St. David's, Paul has evolved from raising his own free-range, corn fed chickens to negotiating contracts with local growers for top quality birds. Paul specializes in capon, a 7-pound rooster chicken considered the crème-de-la-crème of chickens. These birds boast loads of flavour to the delight of his large base of individual customers. In fact, Paul holds a few 'chicken parties' each year to showcase the benefits of using the entire bird from roasting to soup simmering.

To buy from Kent Heritage Farms you must be on their mailing list call the 'chicken diva' Nancy Broerse at 905-262-6021 or email chicken@niagara.com.

SERVES:
6

SEASON:
December,
January,
February

SERVE WITH:
Jackson Triggs
Proprietors
Grand
Reserve White
Meritage,
www.
jacksontriggs
winery.com

vineyard leg of lamb

1 7-pound (3.18 kg) Ontario leg of lamb
2 garlic cloves, sliced
2 sprigs fresh rosemary, destemmed
1/2 cup (125 mL) Kittling Ridge Niagara Bench Small Cask Bandy, Vineyard Series
salt and freshly cracked black pepper
1/2 cup (125 mL) Ontario pinot noir

Using a knife, make small slits all over the lamb and insert garlic slivers and rosemary leaves.
Soak a cheesecloth or tea towel in brandy and wrap around lamb.
Cover with plastic wrap and marinate, refrigerated for 4 hours.
When ready to cook, preheat oven to 450F (230C).
Unwrap the lamb and place fat side up on a roasting rack in a roasting pan.
Season with salt and pepper.
Roast for 30 minutes.
Reduce heat to 350F (180C).
Using a basting brush, baste lamb with wine.
Continue to roast, basting frequently for 1 hour or until done. Let stand 10 minutes before carving.

CHAPTER
4

SERVES:
6 to 8

SEASON:
December,
January,
February

SERVE WITH:
Lakeview Cellars
Merlot Reserve
wine,
www.
lakeviewcellars.ca

The Vintners Quality Alliance (VQA) symbol on a bottle of wine is your guarantee of quality and authenticity. It means the grapes used to make the wine were grown in local soils and the wine was produced according to very strict standards. If a wine doesn't meet VQA regulations, it is refused a VQA designation. It means that now more than ever in the industry's 180-year history, you'll find Niagara wines as good as, or even better than imports of equal kind and value, www.vqaontario.com.

vintage pork in meritage au jus

4 thick, juicy pork chops, butterflied
Salt and freshly ground pepper
4 tablespoons (60 mL) unsalted butter
6 tablespoons (90 mL) olive oil
4 shallots, peeled and minced
2 tablespoons (15 mL) fresh sage leaves
1 cup (250 mL) white meritage

Season chops with salt and pepper.
In a large skillet, heat butter and half the olive oil until hot.
Add the pork chops and cook over medium high heat until browned on both sides, about 10 to 12 minutes.
Remove the chops and place them on a warm platter.
Drain the excess oil from the pan.
In the same saucepan, heat the remaining olive oil and sauté the shallots and sage leaves.
When the sage leaves are crispy, remove half of the oil, add the Chardonnay, and reduce over low heat until the sauce thickens.
Pour the sauce over the pork chops and serve with boiled potatoes and lots more butter.

CHAPTER
4

SERVES:
4

SEASON:
December,
January,
February

SERVE WITH:
Hidden Bench
Nuit Blanche,
White Meritage,
www.
hiddenbench.com

page 139

THE NIAGARA CULINARY TRAIL
The Niagara Culinary Trail is an organization formed by a group of local farmers, chefs and winemakers committed to promoting and providing consumer access to Niagara-grown foods. It is Niagara's best resource for local food, local food products, farm to table culinary events and local restaurants featuring dishes prepared with local foods. Their work keeps the dollars circulating in Niagara communities; it keeps farmers farming and keeps their farms a part of the region's natural landscape. Thank goodness, because fresh, local produce tastes better and is better for you.

www.NiagaraCulinaryTrail.com

Niagara
CULINARY TRAIL

tomato vodka chicken

4 chicken breasts, skinless, boneless
1 cup (250 mL) all-purpose flour
salt and freshly cracked black pepper
2 tablespoons (30 mL) Ontario canola oil
2 shallots, minced
2 garlic cloves, minced
3 dried chili peppers
1/2 cup (125 mL) Prince Igor Vodka from
　　Kittling Ridge Winery & Distillery
1 cup (250 mL) chicken broth
3 tablespoons (45 mL) tomato sauce
1 vine ripened tomato, diced
1/4 cup (60 mL) Parmesan cheese
1/2 cup (125 mL) heavy cream

Trim chicken breasts of any fat.
Season flour with salt and pepper and whisk to mix thoroughly. Heat the oil in a large skillet over medium high heat.
Dredge chicken breasts in seasoned flour and place in skillet. Cook until browned on both sides, about 2 minutes per side. Transfer to a platter and keep warm.
Reduce heat to medium and add shallots, garlic and chili peppers to skillet.
Cook until shallots are soft, about 2 minutes.
Add vodka and cook until vodka has almost evaporated, about 4 minutes.
Add broth and tomato sauce and reduce by half again, another 4 minutes.
Finish the sauce by adding diced tomato, Parmesan cheese and cream.
Heat through, then return chicken breasts to the skillet and cook until done, about 5 minutes.

CHAPTER

4

SERVES:
4

SEASON:
August,
September,
October

SERVE WITH:
Legends Estate
Winery Pinot Noir,
www.
legendsestates.com

Award winning Prince Igor Vodka is made from Ontario grains and distilled in Niagara at Kittling Ridge Estate Wines & Spirits. Prince Igor Vodka comes in both Premium (40% alcohol) and Extreme (45% alcohol) versions. Extreme feels more crisp and clean on the palate, perfect for summer drinks while the Premium gives this dish brilliant flavours and an impressive palate impression.

www.PrinceIgorVodka.com

simply desserts

CHAPTER

5

In this hectic, mad world we live in today, we often lose sight of the very essence that promotes our health and well being – the goodness that comes from the earth, in its own time.

apple flan in apple water

1 1/4 cups (310 mL) all-purpose flour
1/2 cup (125 mL) cold unsalted butter,
    cut into ½-inch cubes
1/4 teaspoon (1.5 mL) salt
2 to 4 tablespoons (30 to 60 mL) ice water
6 Northern Spy apples, peeled, cored,
    halved and sliced 1/8-inch thick
1/4 cup (60 mL) sugar
1 cup (250 mL) water
3 tablespoons (45 mL) sugar
2 tablespoons (30 mL) cold butter, sliced

Pulse together flour, butter and salt in a food processor until most of mixture resembles coarse meal or peas.
Add 2 tablespoons (30 mL) of ice water and pulse 2 or 3 times, or just until incorporated.
Add more water if necessary.
Turn dough onto a floured work surface and form into a ball, wrap in plastic wrap and refrigerate at least 20 minutes.
Meanwhile, wash the apples well, pat them dry and peel them, reserving the apple peelings.
To make apple water, put apple peelings in a medium-size pot and add 1/4 cup of sugar and water.
Bring to a boil and cook for approximately 15 minutes. Strain and set aside.
Preheat oven to 375F (190C). On a lightly floured surface roll out dough into a 13-inch round and fit it into a 10-inch tart tin with a removable bottom and fluted rim, trimming the excess. Brush the bottom of the shell with apple water and arrange the apples decoratively on the pastry shell, overlapping them. Sprinkle sugar on top of the apples, top with butter slices and bake in the middle of the oven for 45 minutes or until the crust is cooked through and the apples are golden.
To serve, puddle apple water on a serving dish and lay a slice of warm apple tart over top.
Makes 1 tart.

CHAPTER
5

SERVES:
8

SEASON:
September,
October,
November,
December

SERVE WITH:
Stoney Ridge
Estate Winery
Igluu, a Select
Late Harvest
Cabernet Franc
Icewine,
www.
stoneyridge.com

page 145

The Duffin family loves apples, they always have. William and Kim Duffin planted the first apple orchard more than 30 years ago and have expanded the farm to 100 acres. Also on the farm are pear trees, peaches, cherries and plums. It's the apple, however, that is their specialty. William Duffin takes the natural approach to farming. "We do everything you can with apples," says daughter Sara. "We eat them, cook with them, press them into juice and cider and of course, we bake a lot of pies."

Duffin Appleworks, 1541 Rice Road, Fonthill.
Farm market is open year round.

cherry brandy angel food cake

1 cup (250 mL) cake flour
3/4 cup (180 mL) sugar
12 egg whites, room temperature
1 teaspoon (5 mL) cream of tartar
1/4 teaspoon (1.5 mL) salt
3/4 cup (180 mL) sugar
2 teaspoons (10 mL) vanilla
1 teaspoon (5 mL) almond extract
1 tablespoon (15 mL) sugar
1 tablespoon (15 mL) cornstarch
1 cup (250 mL) cherry liquid
    drained from sour cherries
3 cups (750 mL) pitted sour cherries
    from Cherry Lane Orchards (juice drained)
1/4 cup (60 mL) Niagara Bench Small Cask
    Brandy, Vineyard Series from Kittling Ridge

Preheat oven to 325F (160C).
In a small bowl, whisk together the cake flour with sugar.
Set aside.
Beat egg whites until frothy; add cream of tartar and salt.
Beat for 1 minute. Add sugar a bit at a time and beat until
soft peaks form, about 2 minutes.
Add the vanilla and almond extract and beat for a few
seconds to distribute evenly.
Sift a quarter of the flour/sugar mixture over the
egg whites and gently fold in.
Repeat until all flour/sugar has been used.
Spoon batter into an ungreased 9-inch tube pan with a
removable bottom. Smooth the top with a spatula and tap
the pan on the counter once or twice to ensure no large
bubbles are present.
Bake for 50-60 minutes, until the top springs back
when lightly pressed.
Remove from oven and invert pan over the neck of a bottle.
Allow to cool completely. Meanwhile, add sugar and
cornstarch to cherry liquid in a saucepan.
Cook over medium heat for 3 minutes, stirring constantly.
Add cherries and brandy. Cook until cherries are warmed
through and sauce begins to bubble. Remove from heat.
Gently run a thin knife around the insides, bottom and
centre tube of the pan to remove the cake.
Set on a cake plate and pour cherry brandy
sauce over cake. Serve warm.

CHAPTER
5

SERVES:
8 to 10

SEASON:
July

SERVE WITH:
Malivoire Wine
Company,
Chardonnay
Musqué Spritz,
www.
malivoirewine
company.com

Two Century Farm is run by Duncan Smith on the basis of
honesty, quality and service. Although Duncan claims his
favourite fruit is whatever is in season, he just cannot resist
the cherry harvest. The sweet ones are great for eating out
of hand, sauces for classic desserts such as this one and his
ultimate favourite has to be the white cherries. Duncan
claims it's the sandy soil that makes his cherries ultra
sweet with a lush palate.

Meet Duncan at the Grimsby Farmers Market
every Thursday from 4:30 to dusk.
www.twocenturyfarm.com
For your fill of sweet cherries, plan on attending the
St. Mark's Anglican Church Cherry Festival in July in
Niagara-on-the-Lake
www.niagaraonthelake.com

concord custard

2 cups (500 mL) seedless Coronation
  Sovereign grapes
1/2 cup (125 mL) sugar
5 farm fresh egg yolks
1/2 cup (125 mL) sugar
2 cups (500 mL) milk
1 teaspoon (5 mL) pure vanilla extract

Wash the grapes, pat them dry and remove from stems.
Squeeze the grape pulp into a medium saucepan,
reserving the skins.
Cook grape pulp until soft, about 10 minutes.
Add the skins and sugar; cook until skins are tender,
about 15 minutes.
Let cool.
Add 1 1/2 cups (375 mL) of milk and purée in a blender.
Pour grape/milk mixture into a medium saucepan and
heat over medium heat until bubbles begin to form
around the edges.
Meanwhile, whisk the egg yolks, sugar and remaining 1/2
cup of cold milk for 3 minutes, or until it becomes lemony
yellow in colour and sugar dissolves.
Remove milk from heat and slowly add a bit of the hot
mixture into the beaten eggs, whisking constantly.
Continue to add hot milk/grape mixture, slowly and in
small amounts until half of it has been added.
Gradually pour the egg mixture into the saucepan with
remaining milk/grape mixture. With a wooden spoon,
constantly stir over medium-low heat until it thickens
enough to coat the back of a spoon, approximately 6
minutes.
Remove from heat and add vanilla.
Pour into 4 small dessert glasses or 8 small liqueur
glasses and cool in the refrigerator until needed.

CHAPTER
5

SERVES:
8

SEASON:
August,
September

SERVE WITH:
Southbrook
Vineyards Vidal
Icewine
www.
southbrook.com

Long before Niagara had a wine industry, concord grapes
like Niagara, Himrod and Coronation Sovereign grew wild
through Niagara. They're not part of the wine grape family
because they're very different. Concord grapes are plump,
juicy, sweet eating grapes, bursting with lots of sweet
grapey flavours. They're the best grape of choice for
making jam, jelly, juice and desserts.

coronation sovereign grape pie

3 cups (750 mL) seedless Coronation
   Sovereign grapes
1/2 cup (125 mL) sugar
4 tablespoons (60 mL) water
1 package unflavoured gelatine
1 cup (250 mL) whipping cream
1 baked 9-inch pie shell
Whole grapes for decoration

Wash grapes, pat them dry and remove from stems.
Squeeze the pulp from the berries into a medium saucepan,
reserving the skins.
Cook grape pulp until soft, about 10 minutes.
Add the skins and sugar; cook until skins are tender,
about 15 minutes.
Let cool and purée in small batches.
Return to the saucepan and add water.
Bring to a boil, remove from heat and stir
in gelatine until dissolved.
Chill mixture for an hour or until thick enough
to mound when dropped from a spoon.
Meanwhile, whip the cream.
When grape purée is completely cooled and
thickened, fold in the whipped cream.
Pour into pie shell and top with whole grapes.
Refrigerate at least 2 hours or overnight.
Serve chilled.
Makes 1 pie.

CHAPTER
5

SERVES:
8

SEASON:
August,
September

SERVE WITH:
Joseph's Estate
Wines Winter
Harvest,
second pressing
of their Vidal
Icewine,
www.
josephsestate
wines.com

International photographer turned organic grape grower
Kevin Argue has a passion for growing organic table grapes,
in particular Coronation Sovereign. These ultra-sweet,
seedless blue grapes are one of the first varieties to ripen
each season. Coronation harvest marks the beginning of
grape harvest in Niagara that lasts 8 to 10 weeks depending
on the weather. These plump, delicious table grapes are sold
to organic stores across the province, including the Organic
General Store in Niagara-on-the-Lake. They're best eaten
out-of-hand and make irresistible jam, jelly, juice and
desserts.

icewine semi freddo

1 1/2 cups (375 mL) Niagara icewine
8 yolks from farm fresh eggs
3/4 cup (180 mL) sugar
2 cups (500 mL) whipping cream

Line a 8-inch square cake pan with cling film.
Over medium high heat, bring icewine to a boil and
reduce to 1 cup (250 mL).
Meanwhile, in a large bowl whisk yolks and sugar until thick
and creamy, approximately 5 minutes.
Add reduced hot icewine to egg yolk mixture by drizzling
very slowly and whisking yolk mixture constantly.
Set aside to cool completely.
When completely cool, whip the cream until stiff peaks form
then gently fold into the icewine egg mixture.
Pour into the lined baking pan and freeze for 5 to 6 hours.

CHAPTER
5

SERVES:
6

SEASON:
January

SERVE WITH:
Inniskillin Wines
Riesling Icewine,
www.inniskillin.
com

In 1984, Inniskillin Wines left a few rows of grapes on the
vine long after harvest. The cold winds stripped the vines of
their leaves and the frigid weather froze the grapes time
and time again. Each freeze and thaw dehydrated the
grapes concentrating the flavours and one late night in
January, the snow was wiped away from the frozen grapes,
they were snapped off the frigid vines and pressed outside
in sub-zero temperatures. The glistening, thick juice was
bottled and history was made. It is marvellous.

Don't miss the Niagara Icewine Festival that takes place in
late January, www.niagarawicewinefestial.com

page 153

late harvest apple strudel

3 tablespoons (45 mL) Greaves
   apricot Jam
3 tablespoons (45 mL) Special Select
   Late Harvest Vidal
4 Ontario Crispin apples, peeled,
   cored and sliced
1 cup (250 mL) brown sugar
1 sheet frozen puff pastry, thawed
1 farm fresh egg
3 tablespoons (45 mL) whole milk
Coarse sugar for sprinkling

Preheat oven to 400F (200C).
Line a baking sheet with parchment paper.
Mix apricot jam and Special Select Late Harvest Vidal
together until smooth.
Mix apples in a large bowl with brown sugar and
apricot/wine mixture.
Set aside.
Place puff pastry on baking sheet.
Roll lightly with a rolling pin into a long rectangle.
With long side of the pastry toward you, arrange
apple filling down the middle.
Fold the pastry lengthwise around the apple mixture.
Seal edges of pastry by dabbing them with water and
pressing the pastry edges together.
Whisk egg and milk together and brush on top of pastry.
Sprinkle with coarse sugar and score the top several times.
Bake for 35 to 40 minutes, or until golden brown.
Makes 1 strudel.

CHAPTER
5

SERVES:
6

SEASON:
October

SERVE WITH:
Henry of Pelham
Winery 2006
Special Select
Late Harvest
Vidal,
www.henryof
pelham.com

NEW VINTAGE NIAGARA
It's a festival to celebrate the release of the year's new wines and the ritual of being among the first to taste Niagara's newest vintage. More than 30 wineries welcome visitors with tours, tastings and special events that focus not only on local wines, but local foods as well. See how delicious things can be when the Niagara Wine Festival partners with the Niagara Culinary Trail to pair the local foods and wines –
it's called regional cuisine.

www.niagaranewvintagefestival.com.

melon granita

1 ripe, fragrant cantaloupe
1/4 cup (60 mL) sugar
Juice of 1 lemon
6 to 8 tablespoons (90 -120 mL) icewine
Slice of cantaloupe for garnish

Cut melon in half and scoop out seeds.
Slice into wedges and cut flesh away from rind.
Put flesh into a food processor with sugar, lemon juice
and icewine, and purée until smooth.
Taste and add more sugar if needed.
Pour the granita mixture into a wide and shallow container,
such as a stainless steel baking dish (the shallower the
container, the quicker the granita will freeze).
Cover and freeze mixture 1 to 2 hours, until it is solid
around the edges.
Take the container out of the freezer and scrape the ice
with a fork, mixing it from the edges into the centre.
Repeat this scraping and mixing process every 30 minutes
or so until the entire mixture has turned into small ice flakes.
When ready to serve, "rake" with a fork to loosen the granita
and spoon into serving dishes and garnish with slice of
fresh cantaloupe.

CHAPTER
5

SERVES:
8

SEASON:
August

SERVE WITH:
Cattail Creek
Family Estate
Winery
Off-Dry Riesling,
www.cattailcreek.
ca

Niagara Fruit Education Centre is on Barton Street right at
the edge of Niagara, built by Llewelyn Smith of the famous
E.D. Smith jam fame. Llewelyn and his family built a large,
modern facility and in it, mix agriculture with culture and
history in a visual story, telling the importance of fruit
farming in Niagara. Inside this giant building you can take a
gardening or cooking class, or browse the towering canvases
of Niagara fruit information. You can even pick your own
cherries from the E. D. Smith cherry orchards. If you're
interested in learning the culture of Niagara agriculture,
it's a great place to be.

Located at 938 Barton Street East in Winona.
www.niagarafruitinstitute.ca

merlot pears with ice milk

4 Bosc pears
3 cups (750 mL) Merlot or other
    dry red wine
1 cup (250 mL) Concord Mountain
    red grape juice
1 cup (250 mL) sugar
2 cinnamon sticks

ICE MILK
4 cups (1 L) whole milk
2 cinnamon sticks
2 teaspoons (10 mL) ground cinnamon
3/4 cup (180 mL) sugar
Mint leaves

Peel the pears and cut off the tops to make lids.
Core the pears and slice the bottoms so they will sit
evenly. Arrange them in a saucepan large enough to hold
them snugly. Add the wine, grape juice, sugar and
cinnamon sticks and cook slowly over medium heat until
the pears are tender, about 20 minutes.
Cool overnight in the syrup.
Meanwhile, combine milk, cinnamon sticks, ground
cinnamon and sugar in a medium saucepan and
bring to a boil.
Let cool slightly and bring to a boil again.
Strain and let cool. Place in an ice cream machine and
process according to manufacturer's directions.
To serve, place each pear on a plate and fill with a
scoop of ice milk.
Top with a lid and garnish with a mint leaf.
Pour approximately 3 tablespoons of Merlot syrup
on the plate around the pear.

CHAPTER
5

SERVES:
4
SEASON:
August,
September

SERVE WITH:
Pillitteri Estates
Winery Cabernet
Franc Icewine,
www.pillitteri.com

page 159

Jane and Don Kouri have operated the 87-acre Concord
Mountain Farm in Grimsby since 1991. When it comes to
harvest all the children and grandchildren help. The Kouris
love their grape juice and grape jelly made from their sun
ripened grapes. The juice is all natural with no preservatives.

Concord Mountain Farm, 324 Thirty Road, RR#2, Beamsville.
You can buy Kouri's grape and apple juice along with their
fruit and vegetables at the Grimsby Farmers Market.

dirty peach cobbler

1 vanilla bean, cut into 1-inch pieces
2 tablespoons (30 mL) all-purpose flour
3/4 cup (180 mL) sugar
5 cups (1.25 L) tree-ripened peaches,
    gently peeled and cut into ½-inch chunks

1 1/2 cups (375 mL) all-purpose flour
1 1/2 cups (375 mL) sugar
2 1/2 teaspoons (12.5 mL) baking powder
1/4 teaspoon (1.5 mL) baking soda
1/2 teaspoon (2.5 mL) salt
4 farm fresh eggs
4 tablespoons (60 mL) whole milk
3 tablespoons (45 mL) peach nectar
1 teaspoon (5 mL) vanilla extract
6 tablespoons (90 mL) unsalted butter,
    melted

Preheat oven to 325oF (160oC).
Process the vanilla bean and flour in a coffee grinder until finely ground.
Put the sugar in a large bowl, add ground vanilla/flour mixture, whisk together. Add peaches and toss to coat.
Transfer mixture to 13 x 9 x 2-inch glass baking dish.
Bake until bubbling, about 25 minutes.
Meanwhile, whisk flour, sugar, baking powder, baking soda and salt in large bowl.
Whisk eggs together with milk, peach nectar and vanilla in medium bowl.
Add wet ingredients to dry ingredients and stir until smooth.
Fold in melted butter.
Pour batter over hot peach mixture.
Return to oven and continue baking until top is golden and tester inserted into centre comes out clean, about 45 minutes longer.
Cool slightly and serve.

SERVES:
12

SEASON:
September

SERVE WITH:
Legends Estate Winery
Goldrich Apricot,
www.
legendsestates.
com

Please...

Don't squeeze me

'til I'm yours!

page 161

Kurtz Orchards Market is Niagara's gourmet farm market located on the Niagara River Parkway just on the outskirts of the town of Niagara-on-the-Lake. It has been run by the Kurtz family for over half a century. Over 100-acres of orchards and farmland produce strawberries, cherries, peaches, plums, raspberries, apricots, pears and plenty more. Inside the large retail barn are their own home made jams, jellies and preserves, as well as antipasto, chutney and spreads packed with their own label. Pick up a sandwich, enjoy the farm scenery and take home a few jars of preserves from the farm.

Kurtz Orchards Gourmet Market, 16006 Niagara Parkway, Niagara-on-the-Lake.
www.kurtzorchards.com

peach, nectarine and plum pie

3/4 cup (180 mL) sugar
3 tablespoons (45 mL) all-purpose flour
1 teaspoon (5 mL) vanilla
1 teaspoon (5 mL) ground cinnamon
1/4 teaspoon (1.25 mL) ground nutmeg
4 medium red plums, pitted and sliced
4 medium peaches, peeled,
    pitted and sliced
2 medium nectarines, pitted
    and thinly sliced
2 cups (500 mL) all-purpose flour
1/4 teaspoon (1.25 mL) salt
2/3 cup (160 mL) shortening
6 tablespoons (90 mL) ice water
Milk
Sugar

To make the filling, stir together sugar, flour, vanilla, cinnamon and nutmeg in a large bowl.
Add the plum, peach and nectarine slices.
Toss gently until fruit is well coated.
Set filling aside.
To make the pastry, stir together the flour and salt.
Using a pastry blender, cut in the shortening until pieces resemble the size of small peas.
Sprinkle 1 tablespoon of water over part of the flour mixture, then gently toss with a fork.
Repeat, using a tablespoon of water at a time, until all is moistened.
Divide dough in half and form each half into a ball.
On a lightly floured surface, roll dough to a 12-inch circle.
Ease pastry into the pie plate, being careful not to break it.
Pour fruit into the pie crust.
For top crust, roll the remaining dough into a 12-inch circle. Cut into ½-inch strips and lay lattice fashion on top of the fruit filling. Trim the pastry even with rim of pie plate, press edges together.
Brush with milk and sprinkle with sugar.
Bake in a 375F (190C) oven for 25 minutes.
Rotate pie in oven and bake for 20 to 25 minutes more or until top is golden.
Remove from oven and cool pie on a wire rack.

CHAPTER

5

SERVES:
8

SEASON:
August

SERVE WITH:
Chateau des
Charmes Wines
2006
Late Harvest
Riesling,
www.chateau
descharmes.com

Steve Pohorly is the third generation to farm the family's two plots of land with his parents, Frank and Sue. One farm is on Niagara Stone Road and it's here, right next to Hillebrand Estate Winery that you'll find their market store offering fruit and vegetables from the farm, including strawberries, cherries, nectarines, tree-ripened peaches, white flesh peaches, eating grapes, apples, prunes and pears and plenty of just-picked vegetables. It's here you'll find delicious tree-ripened peaches.

Open seasonally from June to October,
9 am to 5 pm, weekends until 7 pm.
The Fruit Shack, 1267 Niagara Stone Road,
Niagara-on-the-Lake.

plum tart

1 cup (250 mL) all purpose flour
1/2 teaspoon (2.5 mL) baking powder
1/2 cup (125 mL) unsalted butter,
    room temperature
1/4 cup (60 mL) sugar
1 farm fresh egg
3 plums, halved and cored
1 1/2 teaspoons (7.5 mL) ground cinnamon
3 tablespoons (45 mL) sugar
1/4 cup (60 mL) apricot jam
1 tablespoon (15 mL) water

Heat oven to 350F (180C).
Butter a long 14 x 4-inch rectangular tart pan and set aside.
Combine the flour and baking powder and whisk to blend.
Cream butter and sugar at high speed in a large bowl
of an electric mixer.
Lower speed to medium, add egg and beat until
incorporated.
Gradually add the flour mixture. The dough will be very soft.
Push the dough into the pan with floured fingers to form
an even crust.
Arrange the plum halves in the tart, cut side down.
Mix the cinnamon and sugar together and sprinkle
over the tart.
Bake until the crust is golden brown, about 45 minutes.
Remove from oven and let cool.
Heat the apricot jam and water in a small saucepan over
medium low heat, mixing until combined.
Remove from heat and brush gently over the entire tart.
Makes 1 tart.

CHAPTER
5

SERVES:
6

SEASON:
August,
September

SERVE WITH:
Peller Estates
Signature Series
Ice Cuvee Rose,
www.peller.com

Rene and Eva Schmitz run Palatine Fruit in
Niagara-on-the-Lake. On the 56-acre farm they harvest
strawberries, cherries, peaches, pears and more than a dozen
different varieties of plums. Eva recommends blue plums for
baking, particularly the Ozark or Santa Maria variety because
they have more tartness to balance the sweetness. "They're
just better for baking," says Eva. Blue plums are harvested
mid-August and last until mid-September. Stanley and Early
Italian plums are best for canning. You can find all these
varieties and more at their fruit stand on the farm.

Palatine Fruit on 2108 Four Mile Creek Road,
Niagara-on-the-Lake, 905-468-8627

page 165

potted peaches

3 tablespoons (45 mL) sugar
3 tablespoons (45 mL) water
2 cups (500 mL) peaches, peeled, pitted and diced
1 farm fresh egg
1 tablespoon (15 mL) sugar
1 cup (250 mL) mascarpone cheese, room temperature
1/2 cup (125 mL) heavy cream
Peach wedges for garnish

Warm the sugar and water in a saucepan over medium heat until the sugar dissolves.
Add the peaches and remove from heat.
Stir well and let the peaches steep in the sugar water until room temperature.
Strain, reserving liquid and chill in the refrigerator.
Beat the egg and sugar together in a bowl over simmering water just until thick, about 2 minutes.
Remove from heat and add mascarpone cheese; blend well.
Whip the cream until soft peaks form.
Fold the cream and strained, diced peaches into the mascarpone mixture to form a marbled effect.
Spoon into four custard cups and chill well.
When ready to serve, top with a peach wedge.
Makes 4 servings.

CHAPTER
5

SERVES:
4
SEASON:
August

SERVE WITH:
Reif Estate Winery
1996 Vidal Icewine,
www.riefwinery.com

page 167

They absolutely love peaches!
Chester Kowalik and his family began Peach Country Farm to sell produce from their 32-acre mixed orchards 18 years ago. In the heart of peach country and with a passion for peaches, the Kowaliks offer different varieties of peaches along with the glorious white peach, that is ultra sweet – like candy. The market is open 7 days a week in season offering sweet cherries, plums, nectarines and raspberries along with delicious fruit pies and other Niagara products.

Peach Country Farm Market,
4490 Victoria Avenue North, Vineland Station.
www.peachcountryfarmmarket.com

praline ice cream

Nonstick vegetable oil spray
1 cup (250 mL) sugar
2 tablespoons (30 mL) water
2/3 cup (160 mL) black walnuts,
    shelled, toasted and chopped
1 1/2 cups (375 mL) whole milk
1 1/2 cups (375 mL) heavy cream
6 farm fresh egg yolks
1/2 cup (125 mL) sugar
1 teaspoon (5 mL) vanilla

Spray a sheet of waxed paper with nonstick oil spray.
Stir sugar and water in heavy small saucepan over
medium heat until sugar dissolves.
Increase heat to high and boil without stirring until mixture
turns deep amber colour, occasionally swirling pan and
brushing down sides with wet pastry brush, about 5
minutes. Stir in nuts.
Quickly spread on waxed paper.
Cool.
Crush 1 cup (250 mL) praline and set aside.
Break remaining praline into 8 pieces and set
aside to use as garnish.
In a medium saucepan, combine milk and 1 cup of cream.
Cook over medium heat until bubbles form around the
edges of the pan, about 5 minutes.
Meanwhile, whisk egg yolks, sugar and remaining
1/2 cup of cream in a bowl.
Whisk in about 1/2 cup of the hot milk at a time
until most of the milk is used up.
Pour the tempered egg mixture into the saucepan of hot
milk and cook over low heat, stirring constantly until
mixture coats the back of a spoon, about 6 minutes.
Cool, add vanilla and make ice cream according
to manufacturer's instructions.
Just before ice cream is placed in the freezer,
add 1 cup of chopped praline and mix well.
Pack the frozen mixture into a container and
freeze until solid.
To serve, scoop praline ice cream into small
serving bowls and garnish with a wedge of praline.
Makes about 1 quart.

CHAPTER
5

SERVES:
8

SEASON:
November,
December

SERVE WITH:
Cave Spring
Riesling Icewine,
www.cavespring
cellars.com

GROWING LOCAL
In addition to regional farmers growing our food, Niagara's
home-grown passion can be found in its residents. Klaus
Reif of Reif Estate Winery plants 3 gigantic rows of potatoes
because he loves them, Sandra Marynissen of Marynissen
Winery and husband Glen Muir harvest wild morel
mushrooms from their vineyard, in the west end of
St. Catharines they have a community garden where
neighbours plant their own vegetables and the annual
fundraiser 'Plant-a-Row, Harvest-a-Row' encourages
home gardeners to share their bountiful harvest
with the local food bank.

lavender créme brulée

4 cups (1 L) heavy cream
1 tablespoon (15 mL) dried lavender flowers
8 farm fresh egg yolks
1/2 cup (125 mL) sugar
4 tablespoons (45 mL) sugar

Preheat oven to 300F (150 mL).
Butter 8 ramekins or custard cups and set them into a glass baking dish.
In a large, heavy saucepan over medium heat, put cream and the lavender flowers; heat the cream until tiny bubbles appear around the edge of the saucepan.
Remove from heat and allow lavender flowers to infuse with the cream for 30 minutes.
Strain cream mixture through a fine mesh strainer to remove lavender flowers.
Reheat cream over low heat.
In the meantime, whisk together the egg yolks and sugar until light and creamy. Slowly add the hot cream to the egg mixture, whisking continuously.
Divide custard among the ramekins.
Pour hot water into the baking pan to come half-way up the sides of the ramekins.
Bake 1 hour or until set around the edges but still loose in the centre.
Remove from oven and leave in the water bath until cooled. Remove cups from water bath and refrigerate at least 2 hours.
When ready to serve, sprinkle sugar over each custard. For best results, use a small hand-held torch and hold the torch 4 to 5 inches from the sugar, maintaining a slow and even motion. Stop torching just before the desired degree of doneness is reached, as the sugar will continue to cook for a few seconds after flame has been removed. If you don't have a torch, place custards 6 inches below the broiler for 4 to 6 minutes or until sugar bubbles and turns golden brown. Refrigerate créme brulée at least 10 minutes before serving.

SERVES:
8

SEASON:
July,
August

SERVE WITH:
Sunnybrook Farm Estate Winery Bosc Pear Wine,
www.
sunnybrook
farmwinery.com

Debbie Weicha and her husband Jim run Weicha Farms on Larkin Road in Niagara-on-the-Lake. Besides their prized raspberries, gooseberries and blackberries, Debbie has a passion for growing lavender. She makes vintage sachets and fills them with beautifully-scented dried lavender. Her favourite culinary use for lavender is roasting with lamb or mixing lavender with other savoury spices to make her own 'herbs d'Provence'.

There is no retail store on the farm so call first, 905-468-7482

caramelized rhubarb cake

1 cup (240 mL) granulated sugar
2 tablespoons (30 mL) fresh lemon juice
3 cups (755 mL) rhubarb stalks,
    cleaned and cut into ¼ inch slices
37 ladyfingers
2 tablespoons (30 mL) Kittling Ridge
    Icewine and Brandy
1/2 cup (120 mL) chilled heavy cream
3 tablespoons (45 mL) confectioner's sugar

Put sugar and lemon juice in a saucepan over medium heat and cook until it just begins to brown, about 2 minutes.
Add rhubarb and cook over medium high heat until rhubarb exudes its juices, about 3 minutes.
Remove from heat and cool to room temperature.
Brush flat side of ladyfingers with icewine and brandy.
Lightly oil mould and line with plastic wrap.
Line sides and bottom of mould with ladyfingers, flat sides facing inward and trimming bottom ones to fit snugly.
Beat together cream and sugar until firm peaks form.
Spoon half of rhubarb into mould, smooth top then spoon half of cream over that, smoothing top again.
Cover cream with a layer of ladyfingers.
Repeat layering with remaining rhubarb, cream and ladyfingers.
Cover the top of mould with plastic wrap and chill for 1 day.
Unfold plastic wrap and invert the mould onto a platter.
Serve immediately.

CHAPTER
5

SERVES:
8

SEASON:
May,
June

SERVE WITH:
Kittling Ridge
Estate Wines &
Spirits Icewine
and Brandy
www.
KittlingRidge.com

page 173

Greaves began making pure old-fashioned jams, jellies and condiments in 1927. Owner Angela Redekopp is so particular that she insists only the finest fruits, vegetables and spices are used. The Greaves retail shop is an icon on the main street of Niagara-on-the-Lake, and is the same location they once made their jam from. Today it serves as a retail shop with the full line of Greaves products, while upstairs is a quaint bed and breakfast offering a country experience complete with the flavour of a Niagara summer.

Greaves Jams, 55 Queen Street, Niagara-on-the-Lake.
www.greavesjams.com

strawberry patch pie

3/4 cup (180 mL) butter,
   at room temperature
3 tablespoons (45 mL) fruit sugar
1 teaspoon (5 mL) verjus
1 1/2 cups (375 mL) all-purpose flour
3 sticks rhubarb, cut into 1-inch pieces
1/2 cup (125 mL) sugar
1/2 cup (125 mL) water
1/2 cup (125 mL) sugar
4 cups (750 mL) Niagara strawberries,
   washed and hulled
1 teaspoon (5 mL) cornstarch
2 tablespoons (30 mL) cold water

In food processor, combine butter, sugar and verjus.
Pulse until well incorporated.
Add flour and process until mixture holds together.
Turn out on to floured surface and gently knead until
mixture forms a ball.
With floured fingertips, press dough into 9-inch
(23 cm) pie plate.
Place in freezer for 20 minutes.
Preheat oven to 400F (200C).
Remove pie from freezer and bake for about 12 minutes
or until golden.
Let it cool completely on rack.
Place cut rhubarb and sugar in a saucepan and heat
until rhubarb begins to release liquid.
Stir and bring to a boil until sugar dissolves, about 1 minute.
Turn heat down and simmer for 10 minutes.
Remove from heat and cool in the refrigerator.
When completely cool, spread rhubarb on the bottom of
the pie shell and refrigerate.
In a saucepan, add water and sugar. Heat over high until
sugar dissolves, about 2 minutes.
Set aside.
Meanwhile, arrange the best looking strawberries in the shell
and reserve the rest, fitting them snugly and slicing others
to fit in.
Add remaining strawberries in a blender with sugar water
and blend until puréed.
Pour strawberry purée into the saucepan to heat.
Mix cornstarch in water and pour into sugared strawberries.
Simmer until thickened, about 3 minutes.
Pour over strawberries in pie.
Refrigerate until ready to serve.

CHAPTER
5

SERVES:
8

SEASON:
May, June

SERVE WITH:
Angels Gate
Winery
Snow Angel
Late Harvest
Cabernet,
www.
angelsgate
winery.com

There is a tiny little fruit stand on Lakeshore Road in
St. Catharines. In the back is a kitchen the size of a postage
stamp where Cathryn Ferretti of Nokara Farm pumps out
dozens of fresh strawberry pies to a loyal following every
strawberry season. Huge bowls of plump, juicy strawberries
are picked from the 2-acre strawberry patch not more than
15-feet away. They're washed, hulled and stacked into
baked pie shells. Get there early to get one.

Nokara Farm, 1090 Lakeshore Road West, St. Catharines.
Open daily in season. They also grow peaches, pears,
apricots and a variety of vegetables.

strawberry soup with
pound cake croutons

6 cups (1.5 L) just-picked strawberries,
    cleaned and sliced
1 cup (250 mL) unflavoured yogurt
1 cup (250 mL) table cream
1/4 cup (60 mL) sugar
1 teaspoon (5 mL) pure vanilla extract
1/2 cup (125 mL) Harbour Estates
    Winery Fragole
1 pound cake, cut into 1/2-inch cubes
6 sprigs fresh mint for garnish

Combine the strawberries, yogurt, cream, sugar,
vanilla and fragole in a food processor or blender,
process until smooth.
Chill for one hour.
In the meantime, place the pound cake cubes
on a baking sheet.
Toast for 6 minutes under the broiler,
turning once to brown on 2 sides.
To serve, pour the soup into small chilled bowls
and garnish with the toasted pound cake croutons
and mint sprigs.

CHAPTER

5

SERVES:
6

SEASON:
May, June

SERVE WITH:
Harbour Estates
Winery Fragole,
www.hewine.com

page 177

Doug and Karen Whitty are passionate farmers with an
environmentally friendly sensibility. I remember it as if
it were yesterday. Karen treated me to a tasting of
different strawberries. Just as you taste a variety of
wines, we tasted the different varieties of strawberries
that grow in the Whitty strawberry patch. Some had a
tart edge and would make delicious jam, others were
sweet and delicious - best eaten as you pick them. In
their market they sell what is harvested from their
farm – a mix of fruit and blend of different vegetables
and complement it with the produce from neighbouring
farms.

Whitty Farm Market, 1973 Seventh Street, St Catharines.
The farm market is open during the season from Monday
to Saturday, June to October.

whisky potted maple brioche

PRALINE
Nonstick vegetable oil spray
1 cup (250 mL) sugar
2 tablespoons (30 mL) water
1/2 cup (125 mL) pecans,
    toasted and chopped

MAPLE WHISKY SAUCE
1/2 cup (125 mL) sugar
2 tablespoons (30 mL) water
1/2 cup (125 mL) Niagara maple syrup
4 tablespoons (60 mL) Kittling Ridge
    Forty Creek Whisky
1/2 cup (125 mL) toasted pecans, chopped

BREAD PUDDING
4 large eggs
2 cups (500 mL) whipping cream
1/2 cup (125 mL) sugar
1/2 cup (125 mL) maple whisky sauce
1 teaspoon (5 mL) pure vanilla extract
1 loaf brioche, torn into bite-size pieces

TO MAKE THE PRALINE:
Spray a sheet of waxed paper with nonstick spray.
Stir sugar and water in heavy small saucepan over medium heat until sugar dissolves.
Increase heat to high and boil without stirring until mixture turns deep amber colour, occasionally swirling pan and brushing down sides with wet pastry brush, about 5 minutes.
Stir in nuts.
Quickly spread on waxed paper. Cool.
Chop praline into small pieces.
Store in airtight container at room temperature.

TO MAKE MAPLE WHISKY SAUCE:
In a small saucepan bring sugar and water to a boil.
Add maple syrup and bring back to a boil.
Stir in whisky and toasted pecans.
Remove from heat and allow to cool.

TO MAKE BREAD PUDDING:
Whisk eggs, cream, sugar, maple whisky sauce and vanilla in large bowl to blend.
Add brioche; stir to coat.
Let stand at room temperature 1 hour, stirring occasionally.
Preheat oven to 375°F (190C).
Butter 13 x 9 x 2-inch baking dish or 8 ramekins.
Transfer brioche mixture to prepared dish or individual ramekins.
Bake until golden and toothpick inserted into centre comes out clean, about 40 minutes. Cool slightly.
To serve, garnish with praline and drizzle with maple whisky sauce.

CHAPTER
5

SERVES:
8
SEASON:
December,
January,
February

SERVE WITH:
Hernder Estate
Winery
Blue Bottle
Chardonnay,
www.hernder.com

page 179

Brioche is the richest of breads that gourmands say, can "charm the pants off the fussiest of bread eaters." It's rich and irresistibly buttery yet at the same time has a lightness that belies its rich ingredients.

There are few bakers in Niagara that bake brioche and my two favourites are pastry chef extraordinaire, Catherine O'Donnell of Willow Cakes & Pastries in Niagara-on-the-Lake (www.willowcakesandpastries.com) and the baking diva, Anna Olsen of Olsen's Bakery + Foods in Port Dalhousie (www.olsenbakery.com). You should get to these bakery/ coffee houses early because they tend to run out.

harvest schedule

fresh ▓ from storage ░

Legend: ■ = fresh ▫ = from storage

Fruit	Jan	Feb	Mar	Apr	May	June	July	Aug	Sept	Oct	Nov	Dec
apples	▫	▫	▫	▫	▫		■	■	■	▫	▫	▫
apricots							■	■				
blueberries							■	■	■			
cherries - sweet							■	■				
cherries - sour							■	■				
currants - black + red							■	■				
gooseberries							■	■				
grapes								■	■	▫		
muskmelon								■	■			
nectarines								■				
peaches							■	■				
peaches - Freestone								■				
pears	▫							■	■	▫	▫	▫
plums							■	■	■			
raspberries							■	■				
strawberries						■	■					
tayberries							■	■				

Vegetables

Vegetable	Jan	Feb	Mar	Apr	May	June	July	Aug	Sept	Oct	Nov	Dec
asparagus				■	■							
beans						■	■	■	■	■	▫	
beets	▫	▫	▫	▫			■	■	■	▫	▫	▫
broccoli							■	■	■	■		
brussel sprouts									■	■	▫	
cabbage	▫	▫					■	■	■	■	■	■
carrots	▫	▫	▫	▫	▫		■	■	■	▫	▫	▫
cauliflower							■	■	■	■		
celery							■	■	■	▫		
corn								■	■	▫		
cucumber	▫					■	■	■	■	▫		
eggplant								■	■	■		
garlic	▫	▫					■	■	■	■	▫	▫
leeks	▫							■	■	■	■	■
lettuce						■	■	■	■	▫		
mushrooms	■	■	■	■	■	■	■	■	■	■	■	■
onions - spring					■	■	■	■	■			
onions - cooking	▫	▫						■	■	■	■	▫
parsnips	▫	▫	▫							■	■	■
peas							■	■	■			
peppers								■	■	■		
potatoes	▫	▫	▫	▫					■	■	■	■
radicchio								■	■	■		
radishes					■	■	■					
rhubarb				■	■	■	■					
spinach						■	■	■	■	■		
squash	▫	▫							■	■	■	■
tomatoes								■	■	■	▫	
zucchini							■	■	■	■		

Niagara produce is best eaten fresh during harvest season,
but there are some fruits and vegetables that store well.
They're held in temperature controlled storage warehouses
and allow us to eat Niagara produce longer.

Niagara Cooks is about protecting our farmland and water, its about keeping the farming traditions and cultures in Niagara alive and also about providing our communities with good food.

Niagara's farmers' markets

Each town, village and city has a farmers' market, they're all different and they're a convenient way to purchase local produce.
More than that, it's an opportunity to get to know the people who grow the food you eat.
It's an unbroken arc from the garden to the table that includes growing, harvesting, preparing, presenting and eating foods
from the local soils.

Dunville Farmers' Market
Tuesday and Saturday
7 am to 12 noon

Grimsby Farmers' Market
May to October, Thursday only
4:30 pm to dusk

Niagara Falls Farmers' Market
May to October, Saturday only
8 am to 12 noon

Niagara-on-the-Lake Farmers' Market
May to October, Saturday only,
8 am to 12 noon

Pelham Farmers' Market
May to October, Thursday
4:30 to dusk

Port Colborne Farmers' Market
Friday
6 am to 1 pm
year round

Smithville Farmers' Market
mid-May to mid-October
Saturdays
from 7:30 am

St Catharines Farmers' Market
Tuesday, Thursday and Saturday
5:30 am to 4 pm
all year round

Welland Farmers' Market
Wednesday and Saturday
6 am to 12 noon
all year round
indoor and outdoor

In keeping with the local theme of *Niagara Cooks*, this book was printed in Canada. It would have been easy to have it printed off-shore. In fact it's astonishing how inexpensive it would have been. But if that were the case, the message of eating and buying local would be meaningless. So I paid the extra costs, made *Niagara Cooks* a truly Canadian product and I have to say I'm feeling pretty good about it.

The ability to promote buying and eating local with a local publication was a challenge I was not able to do without help. It is a shame we are loosing our ability to produce Canadian products in a country so rich in resources. It was the commitment and belief of these champions that made it possible to print in Canada.

Together we all believe that buying local creates healthy communities with strong employment and opportunities for growth.

Niagara Cooks is published in Canada thanks to the following most brilliant independent business thinkers in the region.

Buy from them, they excel in service and are passionate about our community.

They made it possible to produce a Canadian product.

Sodexo Canada
Chris Roberts, Resident District Manager
www.Sodexoca.com
We understand the importance of agriculture to this region and are proud to be partners with those who are making the efforts to sustain and revitalize.

Brock University
Director of Community Services, Tom Arkell
St. Catharines, L2S 3A1, 905-688-5550, ext 3749
www.brocku.ca
Brock University is pleased to interact with the Niagara region as a cultural, academic and recreational centre. Leading the way with a strong sense of community, innovation, and excellence, Brock is dedicated to fostering an environment that serves our community both within and outside of Brock.

City of St. Catharines Mayor, Brian McMullan
50 Church Street, St. Catharines, L2R 7C2, 905-688-5600
www.stcatharines.ca
New to the office as of 2007, Mayor McMullan brings with him a new, fresh approach that is invested in revitalizing Niagara communities with St. Catharines at its core. This brilliant and progressive thinking will lead the region into a greater sense of community for us all.

Elmwood cabinetry and design
Brian Daley
443 Eastchester Avenue, St. Catharines, L2M 6S2, 905-688-9770
4104 Fairview Street, Burlington
www.elmwoodniagara.com
When there are thoughts of a new kitchen or bathroom the name Elmwood just rolls off the tongue. Elmwood is a Niagara based company pure and simple and is fully supportive of Niagara's local economy. Mr. Daley says "Niagara's products compare with the finest made or produced anywhere in the world."

Hope & Harder Insurance
512 Welland Avenue, St. Catharines, L2M 5V5, 905-685-1304
www.hopeharder.com
With roots dating back to 1954 and built on a foundation of customer satisfaction and service, Hope & Harder insurance company is a firm believer in agriculture and small business for Niagara. The firm is proud of its many long-term relationships with Niagara residents and is continually building more.

McNamara & Reynolds
28 Nihan Drive, St. Catharines, L2N 1L1, 905-934-7978
From paint to blinds and carpet, this 87-year old company has been passionate about local through three generations. They're secret? Offer excellent quality, at competitive prices, by a team of experienced experts.

buy local champions

Niagara Restaurant Supply Ltd.
17 Lloyd Street, St. Catharines, L2S 2N7, 905-685-8428
www.niagararestaurantsupply.com
For over 30 years, Niagara restaurant supply have helped local businesses build and grow through their philosophy of exceptional service and professional talent. Today, in addition to their business support services, they've opened their doors to home cooks who want restaurant quality culinary tools to work with in their kitchen.

Vintage Hotels
155 Byron Street, Niagara-on-the-Lake, L0S 1J0, 905-468-7738
www.vintage-hotels.com
The family of Four Diamond hotels in Niagara-on-the-Lake that include the Prince of Wales, Queens Landing and the Pillar & Post are proud supporters of the local movement happening in Niagara. Our restaurants continue to increase their purchasing from local farmers.

Nickerson Home Appliances
50 Russel Avenue, St. Catharines, L2R 1V5, 905-685-9075
www.nickersonsappliances.com
In 1954 Don Nickerson opened a small shop repairing washing machines. Thanks to a community that values its resources, today Nickerson's has become a household name for all appliance needs. Always at the forefront of progressive business, Charlie Nickerson is one of the more vocal 'buy local' champions.

St. Davids Hydroponics
822 Concession 7, RR #4, Niagara-on-the-Lake, L0S 1J0, 905-685-3838
www.stdavidshydroponics.ca
The acres of glass on the agricultural horizon is an important contribution to the regions agriculture. Just as picking the right pepper makes a difference, so do all other purchasing decisions. It's a business that's grown in Niagara and is fully committed to the buy local philosophy.

The Furniture Gallery, Frank DiPalma
175 Dieppe Road, St. Catharines, L2M 7S2, 905-685-6184
www.furnituregallery.com
A successful family owned business since 1975. The Furniture Gallery sits in a beautiful building on (175 Dieppe Road, North Service Road) along the QEW in St. Catharines. The DiPalma family pride themselves on the relationships they've build over the years and their community involvement that have made them Niagara's furniture destination. They are perfect examples of how engaging in local business is a successful strategy.

Vineland Research & Innovation Centre, Chair, Donald Ziraldo
www.vinelandontario.ca
The quintessential leader in Niagara, Donald Ziraldo thinks nothing of championing a project targeted at buying and eating local. Take up his 'Buy Local Challenge' available at www.niagaraculinarytrail.com and become part of Niagara's remarkable team to create healthy communities and revitalize our rural landscape.

AG @ Sterling Inn, Faisal Merani
5195 Magdalen Street, Niagara Falls, L2G 3S6, 289-292-0005
www.sterlingniagara.com
Foodies travel far and wide for a taste of AG. Inspired by the growers and producers mentioned throughout this book, AG's menu utilizes regional and seasonal ingredients, brought together by the inventive hand of executive chef, Cory Linkson.

Grape Growers of Ontario
www.grapegrowersofontario.com
Ontario's grape growers, passionate stewards of Niagara's agricultural lands and persistent in their pursuit of excellence in grape growing and in quality grapes produced across Ontario's 15,000 acres of unique vineyards, remain committed to producing the best so that the "buy local" is both a credible and respected initiative for both growers and consumers. The endless acres of vineyards in Ontario and the diversity of products that come from them promote healthy communities and drive a market economy that benefits the consumer and the Niagara region as well as Niagara's reputation nationally and internationally.

**From quick weekday lunches, snacks and suppers
to sophisticated dinner parties, in *Niagara Cooks* you'll find a feast
of delicious dishes you can make no matter where you are.**

index

Lynn Ogryzlo has a weakness for good food.

A second generation Canadian born Italian, Lynn's culinary passion led her into the seductive world of food and wine. She worked with Inniskillin Wines for the first 10 years before branching out on her own as a food columnist. Over the next decade Lynn created more than 1,400 recipes, mostly dedicated to the seasons of Niagara and its food. She was trained as a sommelier, added wine columnist to her credit and introduced her readers to international destinations through their food and drink. In addition to writing, Lynn became culinary host on CHCH-TV's Niagara Express, focusing solely on Niagara's culinary wealth. Lynn's energy and creativity drove her to found the Niagara Culinary Trail so home cooks, chefs and visitors to the region could have access to local foods, whether by shopping at farm stands or enjoying a seasonal restaurant meal, www.NiagaraCulinaryTrail.com

Though she is a contributing author on a number of books, this is Lynn's long-awaited first cookbook. It's a way of sharing with all who believe that a better quality of life comes not from accumulating material possessions but in surrounding oneself with the very best flavours at their peak of ripeness.

Lynn and Jon Ogryzlo are a husband-and-wife team who have inspired each other for almost three decades. A talented photographer, Jon creates magic through the lens and makes food on the plate entice and excite.

Through the pages of this cookbook, you'll find quick and easy recipes that will whet your appetite for the lighter flavour of fresh foods, sources for obtaining local ingredients and wine pairings that make it easy to create your own local meals to share with family and friends.

We invite you to explore Niagara's regional cuisine and Niagara's award-winning VQA wines.

These are surely experiences to make any palate tingle!

page 191

Lynn O.

Lynn Ogryzlo
www.niagaracooks.com

what it's all about

Eating local is about buying local.
Buying local is about more than buying food.
Eating and buying local is about keeping our
hard earned dollars circulating in our community.

Niagara Cooks is about the Niagara community
and its message is one of choice.

We have all discovered the high cost of
cheap food and goods is more than we can bear.

Buying local is Niagara's answer to the global crisis.

Knowing we have a choice,
why would anyone choose to be cheap, fast and easy?
Making the right decisions about our daily purchases can change our region.

Niagara Cooks therefore, is about more than buying local, it offers hope.
It lays a foundation upon which we can build a new system – a new region.

to be continued . . .

Mixed Sources

Product group from well-managed
forests and other controlled sources

www.fsc.org Cert no. SW-COC-1271

© 1996 Forest Stewardship Council

FSC